# COMBAT LEGEND

# P-51 MUSTANG

## Kev Darling

**Airlife**

Copyright © 2002 Airlife Publishing Ltd

Text written by Kev Darling
Profile illustrations drawn by Dave Windle
Cover painting by Jim Brown – The Art of Aviation Co. Ltd

First published in the UK in 2002
by Airlife Publishing Ltd

**British Library Cataloguing-in-Publication Data**
A catalogue record for this book
is available from the British Library

ISBN 1 84037 357 1

Printed in Hong Kong


*Contact us for a free catalogue that describes the complete range of
Airlife books for aviation enthusiasts.*

**Airlife Publishing Ltd**
101 Longden Road, Shrewsbury SY3 9EB, England
E-mail: sales@airlifebooks.com
Website: www.airlifebooks.com

# Contents

Chapter 1     A Flash of Silver in the Sky:     4
Development History of the P-51

Chapter 2     Into the Wild Blue:     21
Mustang in Service

Chapter 3     Creating the Legend:     37
Mustang People

Chapter 4     Combat Zone:     53
The Fighting Mustang

Chapter 5     Mustangs for all Seasons:     69
Versions and Variants

Appendices     Weapons and Systems     87
Mustang Production
Mustang Survivors
Mustang Models
Mustang Books

Index     96

# Mustang Timeline

**26 October 1940**
Maiden flight of Mustang prototype NA-73X/NX19998

**23 April 1941**
First flight of production of Mustang Mk I AG345

**20 May 1941**
First combat mission with Army Co-operation Command

**16 April 1942**
USAAF orders A-36A Apache

**13 October 1942**
Maiden flight of R-R Merlin-powered Mustang X testbed

**30 November 1942**
Maiden flight of the XP-51B

**April 1943**
A-36A Apache begins combat operations

**September 1943**
P-51As enter service with 14th AF in China

**17 November 1943**
First flight of XP-51D, converted from P-51B

**1 December 1943**
Eighth AF receives its first P-51s

**13 December 1943**
Eighth AF Mustangs begin missions over Europe

**2 April 1944**
Fifteenth AF in Italy receives P-51B Mustangs

**3 February 1945**
First flight of P-51H

**7 April 1945**
P-51D Mustangs begin operations over Japan

**23 April 1945**
Maiden flight of Allison-engined XP-51J

**12 June 1945**
First flight of prototype XP-82 Twin Mustang

**27 June 1950**
F-82G Twin Mustang scores first air victory of Korean War

**7 February 1978**
Last Mustang in US military service retires when US Army aircraft leave Edwards AFB: now on display at Fort Rucker.

**1984**
Dominican Air Force retires last 12 operational Mustangs thus bringing the service history of this long-lived veteran to a close.

# 1. A Flash of Silver in the Sky: Development History of the P-51

Mustang. The very word itself evokes visions of speed, beauty and grace, both of the equine and mechanical kind. In this case, it of course refers to that product of World War Two, the North American Aviation (NAA) P-51 Mustang – built to last for 400 hours and destined to last for 40 years.

The start of the Mustang story begins amid the wreckage of the American aviation industry in the 1930s. The collapse of Wall Street had precipitated a shake-up in the whole industry, which had resulted in the creation of North American Aviation Inc. The location chosen for the new conglomerate was Mines Field in Southern California. It was an already active airfield, had good routes of supply and, most importantly, was available for a knockdown price. Building of the new factory, which covered some 159,000 square feet, began in 1936. Initially employing a workforce that numbered 150 in total, the new company began development of the Model NA-16 that eventually emerged as the Harvard and Texan trainers. Paralleling this development was that of the O-47, destined to be an observation aircraft for the Army Air Corps.

As this was a new company, it suffered the usual range of problems that all new organisations undergo. However, by 1940 under the guidance of company president James H 'Dutch' Kindelberger, North American had become better established and was thus able to extend its range of activities.

Whilst Kindelberger was nurturing North American, events across the Atlantic had already taken a turn for the worse. In September 1939 war had been declared between Britain and Germany after the latter had invaded Poland. Part of the response was to increase fighter production to maintain squadron strength and to build up a small operating reserve. The primary aircraft types involved were the Hawker Hurricane and the Supermarine Spitfire. Both these aircraft shared one primary common denominator, this being the classic Rolls-Royce Merlin engine.

## British requirements

The Royal Air Force had already received some American aid in the shape of Curtiss Tomahawks and Lockheed Hudsons which were barely adequate for the tasks presented to them, whilst the earlier Curtiss Mohawk and Bell Airacobra were even less successful. All of these aircraft had been produced using the renowned American technique of mass-production based around a moving construction line. Given that manufacturing methods in Britain were much less efficient, it is hardly surprising that the RAF was looking to American technology to produce more fighters at a faster rate.

In the United States North American was already gearing up for quantity building of the Curtiss Tomahawk under licence. However, when the British Purchasing Commission (BPC) turned up, Kindelberger managed to persuade them that the Tomahawk was at the end of its design life and that a completely new aircraft would be a better bet.

The new proposal was to be ground-breaking in its concept. This would be a fighter that would incorporate all the latest expertise in air combat that had been hard-learned over the skies of Britain and Europe.

Standing in the way was the American government, which was still nominally operating a policy of neutrality if not isolationism. Therefore, such a proposal needed State Department approval. Given the circumstances it was quite surprising that the required clearances were given very quickly, although the price was two aircraft to be furnished at no expense for evaluation by the United States Army Air Force. Neither of the two major players in this contract saw any problem with this requirement, thus the programme was given the go-ahead.

The first design sketches for the NA-73 were prepared by J L Atwood under the guidance of Kindelberger, and passed to the BPC for approval. This was quickly forthcoming, although the armament specification was revised to eight machine-guns so that it would match that of the Hurricanes and Spitfires already in service. With the weaponry set, the next requirement was speed, not only in design, but in the production of a first prototype, designated the NA-73X. The assigned team of designers took on board the problems that Supermarine had encountered in creating and producing the Spitfire. As a result, every component was designed for easy mass-production and assembly.

## Advanced new wing

Given that North American was already proceeding down the road of innovation, it is hardly surprising that the newly envisioned 'laminar flow' wing was quickly adopted. This aerofoil had been partly developed under the aegis of the National Advisory Committee for Aeronautics (NACA). The theory behind this particular development was to place the centre of air pressure further back on the wing, which in turn delayed the departure of turbulent air until much later. The resultant decrease in drag also improved lift and speed.

Concurrent with the improved wing, the design team also decided to blend the fuselage lines to create a more aerodynamically efficient airframe. This also involved ensuring that, where possible, all components would be hidden under the aircraft's skin.

The chosen powerplant for the NA-73X was the Allison V-1710, which was a liquid-cooled V-12 engine. There were more-powerful engines available from other manufacturers,

Photographed not long after its roll-out, the first prototype NA-73X already exhibits the sleek lines associated with the P-51 Mustang. Of note is the low profile of the under-fuselage radiator that would undergo some revision before the manufacture of production aircraft. *(NAA Archive)*

Prior even to the cutting of metal a mock-up of the NA-73X underwent extensive wind tunnel trials at various establishments, as North American had no facilities to undertake such work. Although the laminar flow wing was found to be effective the application of paint and odd boot mark did reduce its effectiveness slightly. *(NAA Archive)*

but these were all radial in layout. The Allison was the most powerful inline unit available in America, and allowed the designers to retain the smooth clean lines of their aircraft.

## Radiator layout

Having chosen the engine, the next concern to face the design team was the placement of the radiator. Choosing its location was of prime importance, as was the amount of the heat exchange matrix that would have to be extended into the airflow. Too much exposure to the passing slipstream would cancel out all the careful drag reduction work undertaken on the rest of the airframe. The final chosen location was under the fuselage just aft of the cockpit. This was a quite ingenious assembly as it featured a retractable ram scoop, which allowed the maximum cooling air in whilst not overly disturbing the airflow. Externally this whole set-up looked fairly simple, although from the outset the cooling pipes under the skin from the engine to the matrix were recognised as being vulnerable to gunfire.

Although the aircraft looked good on paper the company had neither the experience nor the equipment to evaluate the design in a wind tunnel. To combat this deficiency and to evaluate the new fighter NAA purchased wind tunnel time and data from Curtiss Aircraft. This step would, in later years, give rise to the erroneous supposition that the Mustang was no more than a reworked version of the experimental Curtiss XP-46 design.

## Rapid construction

With most of the design elements in place, the Purchasing Commission placed a letter of intent on 10 April 1940, and the final contract was placed on 23 May. From this period comes the story that NAA would deliver the first prototype for testing within 100 days. In an effort to achieve this seemingly impossible target the employees of the company worked seven days a week, some staying in the factory for sixteen hours a day. All this effort eventually resulted in the roll-out of the NA-73X prototype some 117 days later.

This was more of a publicity gimmick than reality. To speed construction, the wheel assemblies had been borrowed from the T-6 trainer production line, and the engine would not be delivered for another twenty days. But even if it was a gimmick, it was not too far from

The first Mustang looks a sorry sight, upside-down in a field after its fifth flight. Engine failure forced pilot Paul Balfour to make an emergency landing, ground-looping on soft earth after touchdown. In spite of its battered state, NX19998 was repaired and returned to flying. Here, the recovery process has begun with the removal of the engine. Note the painted 'gun ports' on the wing leading edges. *(NAA Archive)*

the truth. Such was the precision with which the prototype had been built that installation of the Allison powerplant was completed without delay, within a day of delivery.

From the beginning it was considered by some members of the design team that the Allison unit was a stand-in until a better engine could be found. A superb performer at low level, its performance fell off rapidly above 11,000 feet, even with full boost emergency war power. In any sort of high-altitude fight like those which were taking place in Europe, such a weakness gave enemy fighter pilots the right to choose the altitude for combat. Nevertheless, the engineers at North American spent a great deal of time ground-running the powerplant to integrate it with the revolutionary cooling system. As this was an aircraft that was 'so right', very few difficulties were encountered and the trials proceeded smoothly.

So smoothly, in fact, that North American set the maiden flight date for October 1940. They immediately ran into a problem, in that they did not have in their employ a qualified fighter pilot. The company did have its own test pilots on the payroll, but their main employment was to test-fly production aircraft prior to delivery.

They had to look outside the company.

This was very much the era of the itinerant pilot in the United States. One of these flamboyant personalities was one Vance Breese. Such was this gentleman's reputation in the field of flight-testing that he was in great demand, hence the rather large fee paid by NAA for his services.

## First Flight

On 26 October the prototype NA-73X was on the NAA ramp surrounded by T-6 trainers. In contrast to the rugged looks of these sturdy machines, the shiny-metal Mustang looked very much the thoroughbred after which it would later be named. Once Breese had settled himself into the cockpit, the process of launching the aircraft began. A run-through of the pre-flight check-list was carried out before the Allison engine was started. In common with all piston engines a few minutes were needed to allow it to warm up to its operating temperature. Given clearance to depart, the pilot released the brakes and opened the throttle to taxi. He immediately came across a problem that was to be common amongst long-cowled, tail-wheeled aircraft, that of not being able to see forward over the engine without weaving the aircraft from side to side.

## No problems

Once on the runway threshold, the brakes were applied and the throttle advanced for take-off. With brakes released a certain amount of rudder was needed to offset the torque of the Allison engine. Although there was a touch of fog around the airfield, the take-off proceeded smoothly, as did the subsequent undercarriage retraction. This first flight was a very sedate, carefully controlled affair, caution being the test pilot's watchword in a brand new design. After about twenty minutes Breese turned back towards Mines Field and landed the NA-73X without any problems. After debriefing, and since no serious flaws had been discovered, the aircraft was cleared for further test flying to expand its flight envelope. Vance Breese made another three flights in the NA-73X before departing to pursue other projects.

His replacement was Paul Balfour, whose connection with the first prototype was to be short-lived. On 20 November the aircraft was cleared for its fifth flight for the purpose of confirming the behaviour and calibration of the airspeed indicator. After a clean, trouble free take-off a series of low-level runs at varying speeds were made over the airfield for the calibrators. It was at the end of one of these fly-bys, at the point of pulling up, that the Allison engine began to exhibit signs of rough running. Realising that he had a problem the pilot attempted to turn back towards the airfield; however, the turn was not completed as the engine failed completely. Left with very few options he turned the aircraft towards a field near Lincoln Boulevard, close to Mines Field. The NA-73X was now a glider. With both the undercarriage and flaps set for a power-off landing, the approach was perfect and a good landing would have been made, had the main wheels not hit a patch of very soft, recently ploughed earth. This was akin to slamming on the brakes, and the result was the same. The NA-73X stopped its landing immediately and promptly flipped over on its back. The saving grace for the pilot was the high rear fuselage, which prevented him from being crushed. As he climbed out of the canopy side window, the aircraft was being drenched by fuel leaking

Two early production airframes were held aside from the British order and were shipped to the US Army Air Corps, where they were given the designation XP-51. Production aircraft differed from the prototype, most obviously in the extended inlet above the engine cowling and the redefined radiator fairing. Although most of the airframe remained unpainted, there was a matt black anti-dazzle panel in front of the windscreen whilst the rudder carried Air Corps-style red, white and blue stripes. *(NAA Archive)*

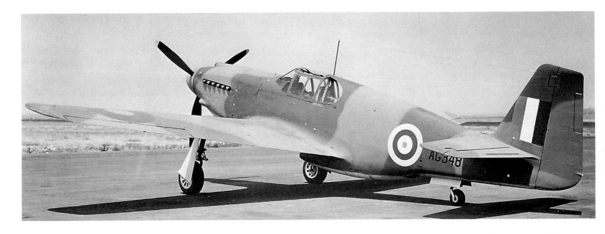

Mustang Mk I AG348 was the fourth production airframe from the BPC contract. It features the original short air intake above the cowling, extended on later aircraft to eliminate airflow problems. The aircraft is seen here after its first flight; it was soon to be dismantled and sent to Britain. *(NAA Archive)*

from the ruptured fuel tanks. The post-crash investigation revealed that the engine had suffered from fuel starvation due to incorrect selection of the next tank in the sequence.

## Back in the air

Although the prototype was a write-off, both the NAA management and the Purchasing Commission officials agreed that overall the NA-73X was the aircraft they were looking for. To continue the flight test programme, it was originally proposed that early production machines be used. However, this option was not exercised as the damaged airframe was recovered from its muddy resting place and returned for rebuilding. This was quickly accomplished, the rebuilt NA-73X making its second maiden flight on 3 April 1941. The pilot on this occasion was R C 'Bob' Chilton, who had replaced the unfortunate Balfour.

As before, the usual sequence of shake-down test flights were carried out before the serious work began again. Overall, the NA-73X carried out a surprisingly limited number of flights, as by now production machines were beginning to leave the factory and the prototype was seen, quite rightly, as not being fully representative of the P-51. Unfortunately the final fate of this particular airframe is unknown. It is possible that it was scrapped without ceremony.

As the first aircraft began to leave the factory, the NA-73X was formally named 'Mustang' by

the BPC. The first Mk I, AG345, undertook its maiden flight on 23 April 1941, the pilot being Louis Watt. By this time North American had established the full production line in its new building, where components built in advance were literally bolted and riveted together before rolling out at the other end as complete aircraft. The initial contract for the Mustang Mk I was for 320 units priced at $40,000 each, although this soon increased to 620. In common with many such purchases the price only covered the basic airframe, the remainder being 'Government-Furnished Equipment'. This list normally included the engine, armament and some associated operating equipment, radio equipment, navigation equipment and many other minor items such as the medical pack.

## British trials

The second production airframe, AG346, was dismantled, crated and shipped to Britain aboard ship. It was unloaded safely at Speke docks, Liverpool, on 24 October 1941. Here it was reassembled and test-flown. Extensive flight tests to evaluate performance and handling were undertaken at the Aeroplane and Armament Experimental Establishment (A&AEE) at Boscombe Down. The pilots assigned to the evaluation programme confirmed that the data already received concerning the NA-73X and the first production machine were correct, and needed no further adjustment in the forthcoming pilot's notes.

This process of delivery became standard as speed was of the essence. Each aircraft, after completing its California test flight, would be disassembled, crated, protected and shipped in convoy to Britain. They did not all arrive, however. Convoys were subject to harassment and attack by U-boats and Focke-Wulf Fw 200 Condor bombers, both of which took their toll in 1941 and 1942. Thus some of the badly needed fighters proceeded no further than the bottom of the Atlantic Ocean.

## High-performance fighter

After arrival in Britain, the new aircraft underwent a series of minor modifications to the ducting system to improve performance. The Mustang was a much faster machine than the Spitfire V at altitudes below 11,000 feet, having a speed edge of 35 mph over the Fighter Command mainstay. Although this was impressive, air combats over Europe normally took place at higher altitudes, putting the early Mustangs at a disadvantage against high-flying Messerschmitt Bf 109s and Focke-Wulf Fw 190s.

Some early examples of the Mustang were sent to RAF Duxford and the Air Fighting Development Unit (AFDU) for evaluation and to identify where the new fighter might be most profitably used. Although it performed well against a captured Messerschmitt Bf 109E at all levels up to 11,000 feet, later models of the 109 and the Focke-Wulf Fw 190 would be more of a challenge, and the high-altitude deficiency was even more marked. The problem with Allison engine performance stopped the Mustang Mk I entering general front-line RAF service.

That is not to say that early Mustangs were redundant. A number were shipped off to the Soviet Air Force, whose war was primarily being fought at low level, whilst others were passed to the Army Co-operation Command. This new organisation had been formed in December 1940. Its primary task was to co-ordinate activities between air and ground forces, a precursor to the modern Forward Air Controller system. Lack of co-ordination had been most noticeable during the time the British Expeditionary Force had spent in France, and the lack of effective air support had made it easier for the German forces to overcome any opposition.

The choice of the Mustang Mk I for this role was made on its merits, these being its low-level speed, armament, manoeuvrability and

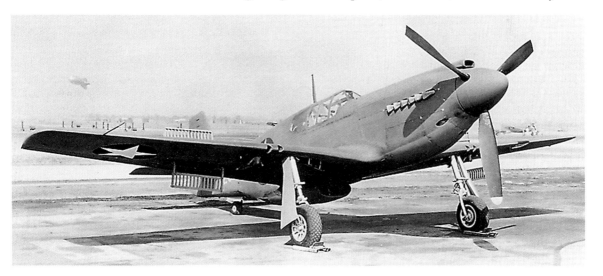

The first US Army order for the new North American fighter was for the A-36A Apache, a dive bomber/ground attack version of the Mustang. Armament included six 0.50-calibre machine-guns, four in the wing and two under the nose firing through the propeller. The main modification to the Apache was the fitting of hydraulically powered airbrakes, seen here fully open. The underwing bomb shackles are also visible. *(NAA Archive)*

range. This was a vast improvement on the Command's original equipment which had included Westland Lysanders and Curtiss Tomahawks. Both were seen as excessively vulnerable in the dangerous skies over occupied Europe.

## US interest aroused

Whilst the Royal Air Force was deciding what to do with its Allison-powered Mustangs the two airframes sequestered for the US Army Air Force were being evaluated by pilots more used to flying the less-than-adequate P-35 and P-36 fighters. Suitably impressed by airframes No. 4 and 10, these pilots passed on their conclusions. This resulted in both aircraft, now designated as XP-51s, being transferred to Wright Field, Dayton, Ohio at the end of 1941.

There they were to be subjected to extensive testing. Prior to their arrival at the Army's primary test base, North American had modified the aileron mounting brackets to increase their stiffness, thus improving the roll control of the aircraft. Test flying of the XP-51 was very low key, as Wright Field was full of new fighter types awaiting evaluation. Some flying was done, but not enough to bring the Mustang into the limelight.

On 7 July 1941 the Purchasing Commission admitted that they were running out of operating capital. As a result, the US government took a decision that was to change the whole war from the British point of view. In order to help the British and to finally bury the tail end of the Great Depression, a policy known as Lend-Lease was instituted. The concept behind this innocuous title meant that America would provide virtually all the armaments required by Britain. However, much was required in exchange, such as the establishment of semi-permanent bases in British overseas possessions. The other main proviso was that all equipment would either be destroyed, returned or paid for at the end of hostilities.

Another change wrought by Lend-Lease was that contracts would be placed by the relevant military service in the USA. Thus, aircraft for the RAF were purchased by the USAAF. The first contract that was effected under this policy was the procurement of a variant known as the

Mustang Mk IA. This had four 20-mm cannon in place of the machine-gun armament of the original Mk I. A total of 150 were ordered, including 55 which were to be retained by the USAAF for evaluation, even though the service had yet to carry out flight-testing of the type.

Although now it possessed two prototypes and fifty-five fighters, the US Army had yet to purchase the type in quantity. Nevertheless, Dutch Kindelberger was determined that he would secure some of the rapidly increasing defence largesse for the Mustang.

The route chosen was not the most obvious. Images from Europe had impressed upon the American armed forces the apparent effectiveness of dedicated dive bombers – although in reality, such machines were very vulnerable to expertly flown fighters. Kindelberger and his team dedicated their time to creating a dive bomber from the Mustang. The most obvious external change was the incorporation of dive brakes above and below the wings, and structural strengthening of the airframe to withstand the increased g forces.

## Dive-bombing Apache

With the design frozen, the NAA management presented their new aircraft to the US Army. Fortunately for Kindelberger the Army decided to order the aircraft as the A-36A Apache. On 16 April 1942, a total of 500 were contracted for by the USAAF, who were exceptionally pleased with their new purchase. Not only was the A-36 capable of delivering its bombs accurately on target, it was more than capable of defending itself after release. The only regret the USAAF was to have was that the order was so small, since hard use would mean that very few survivors were still in service at the end of war.

The development of the Mustang would be rapidly accelerated after 7 December 1941, when the bombing of Pearl Harbor precipitated the United States decisively into the war. One of the first effects of this attack was that the US government ordered vast quantities of fighters from all sources. For NAA this meant that orders for the Allison-powered P-51 Mustang were quickly forthcoming. These retained the original machine-gun armament and were

European combat experience had shown the value of cannon armament in fighters, and a number of early P-51s were tested with four 20-mm cannon. The cordite streaking under the wings indicates that this example, seen being rearmed at Wright Field, has already seen some heavy firing. *(NAA Archive)*

shipped to Britain for use over Europe. Given the altitude limitations, the best use of the P-51 was in the reconnaissance role, for which purpose-designed camera-equipped aircraft were developed and given the designation F-6. Other machines were shipped overseas to India, where they gave excellent service with the Air Commando Groups fighting against the Japanese in China and Burma.

Although the USAAF had ordered 819 examples of the Allison-powered aircraft, their widespread distribution throughout Britain, China, India and the United States meant that there was an overall shortage in each theatre.

This three-quarter rear shot of an early-build P-51 shows the radiator inlet and exhaust in the lowered position. Also, the carburettor inlet atop the engine cowlings is clearly defined. *(NAA Archive)*

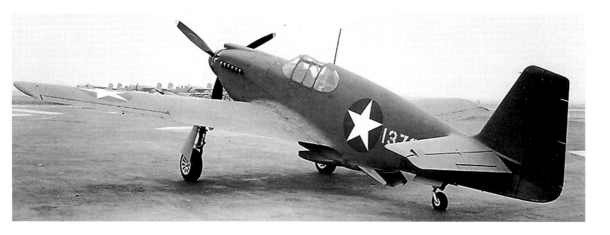

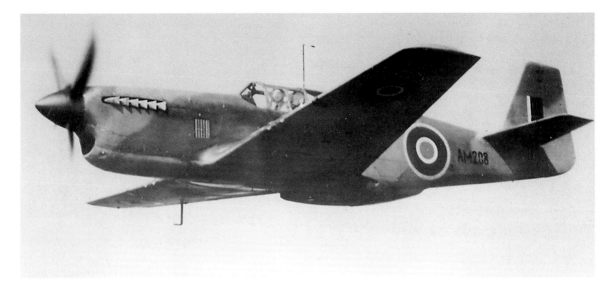

When Rolls-Royce added the Merlin to the Mustang it was originally cooled by an air intake under the nose. In this form it was known as the Mustang X, and three airframes were converted for trials purposes. The resulting aircraft proved to have outstanding potential. *(NAA Archive)*

Also, the limitations of the powerplant were again starting to cause problems in combat.

The first step towards solving the engine dilemma had already been taken. On 30 April 1942, Rolls-Royce test pilot Ron Harker visited the AFDU at Duxford to fly Mustang Mk I AG422. Although altitude-limited, the test flights carried out by Harker inspired him with great enthusiasm for the Mustang. Given its excellent fuel load, manoeuvrability and closely grouped armament, he estimated that if the airframe were fitted with the more fuel-thrifty Merlin, the resulting aircraft should easily be able to reach into the heart of Germany.

For Harker, getting the Merlin fitted to the Mustang airframe was hard work. Much of officialdom was less than enthusiastic about the idea of grafting a British engine onto the front of an American fighter. However, believing in his cause, Harker finally persuaded enough high-ranking personnel to back his proposal. Eventually Rolls-Royce enlisted the aid of Air Marshal Sir Wilfred Freeman, who arranged for three airframes to be delivered to the Rolls-Royce test airfield at Hucknall.

The conversion work was undertaken by Rolls-Royce engineers. They modified the bulkhead engine mounts, reworked the cowlings and revised the cooling system to match the installed Merlin 65. The first flight of AL975/G (the 'G' indicating a need for a constant guard whilst on the ground) was undertaken on 13 October. The pilot was Captain R T Sheppard, who was the Chief Test Pilot at Rolls-Royce.

The results were astounding. The Merlin-Mustang retained the earlier aircraft's superior low-level performance, but now it was as good as, if not better than, any any other fighter at altitude as well. The new machine also promised exceptional range as well as speed and agility.

## Merlin development

The other two airframes were also converted to Merlin power and a full-scale development programme was begun. To wring the most out of the new combination a variety of propellers was tried, cowling shapes were altered, the superchargers were modified and the cooling system was redesigned. These eventually resulted in a truly long-range fighter capable of high speed and great manoeuvrability.

The results were sent back to America by the Air Attaché in London. Lieutenant-Colonel Thomas Hitchcock enthused mightily about the

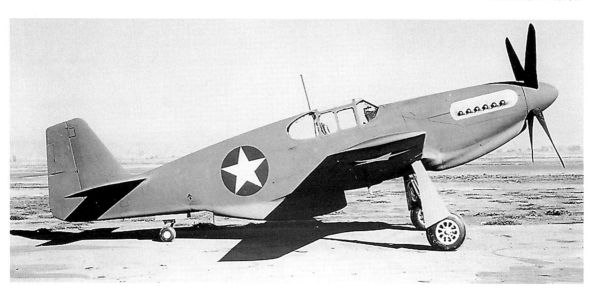

This anonymous Mustang is in fact the XP-51B prototype, complete with an early Merlin installation. Note the deepened intake under the nose. Problems with handling and airflow soon saw this refined to the more familiar shape associated with the Rolls-Royce-powered product. *(NAA Archive)*

new combination, which was good news for the NAA President, Dutch Kindelberger, who had never been overly enamoured of the Allison engine or its manufacturer. Following on from the report sent by the Air Attaché, Rolls-Royce sent data specifics to North American, which enabled them to convince the USAAF that Merlin-engined aircraft should be built in place of those powered by Allisons.

Whilst North American was reworking its production line for the Merlin-powered Mustang, Rolls-Royce was undertaking further development of the type. This concerned the more powerful Griffon engine which eventually would power the Spitfire. Unlike its British counterpart, the Griffon engine mount for the Mustang would be in the centre of the fuselage, very much in the mould of the less-than-successful Bell P-39 Airacobra. This unusual arrangement only ever appeared on the drawing board.

With the tentative agreement of the USAAF, North American contracted Packard to build the Merlin engine in the United States. This decision had two positive ramifications. First, as one of the biggest volume vehicle manufacturers in the country Packard would experience few problems in turning out high

quality products speedily. Second, building in America removed the need to ship everything from Britain, avoiding the attendant dangers from the *Kriegsmarine*'s U-boats that the convoys attracted.

## Packard production

Given the new engine and extensive airframe modifications, it is not surprising that a new designation was applied to the aircraft, this being the XP-87. To hasten the development of the new Mustang a pair of Mk IAs were withdrawn from the Inglewood production line for conversion to the new Packard V-1650-3, rated at 1,520 hp. The American designation for the engines was entirely different to that used by Britain.

The mounting for the new powerplant was completely redesigned from Rolls-Royce's original ideas, being completely revamped, primarily for ease and speed of manufacture. A further set of modifications saw stainless steel fairings blended around the exhaust stubs, whilst the small air intake that had originally been perched above the cowling was moved to the underside of the nose and tidily faired in.

Further modification to the cooling system led to an enlarged radiator scoop containing a

Production moves on apace at the expanded North American plant at Inglewood, as P-51B Mustangs move down the line. Completed Mustang fuselages are mounted on castored construction frames. Demand for the P-51 necessitated the construction of another factory at Dallas in Texas. *(NAA Archive)*

radiator matrix of increased area plus an intercooler. This change resulted in no reduction in the aircraft's performance, since the whole assembly had been aerodynamically refined. To compensate for the growth in engine output, the entire airframe was strengthened. The power generated by the Merlin engine was absorbed by a four-bladed Hamilton Standard Hydromatic propeller unit of 11 foot 2 inch diameter, whilst the fixed armament was set at either four or six 0.50-inch machine-guns (although one of the XP-87s was equipped with four 20-mm cannon for comparison purposes).

## P-51 flies with American Merlin

The first flight of an American-built Merlin-powered Mustang took place from Inglewood on 30 November 1942. In front of a group of VIPs which included General 'Hap' Arnold, the NAA pilot took the aircraft, finished in a scheme of olive drab and neutral grey, through a display that was enough to convince the party that the order already placed for 2,200 of the type was correct.

It was at this time that the USAAF changed the designation to XP-51B to cover the prototypes. Production P-51Bs were built at the expanded Inglewood plant. A new plant was

built at Dallas, Texas where the aircraft, although essentially similar, would emerge as the P-51C. A third and final production facility was later built at Tulsa, Oklahoma which enabled NAA to keep up with the orders for the P-51 fighter, the B-25 Mitchell bomber and the T-6 Texan trainer.

With its new engine and other refinements the new Mustang achieved that rare distinction of exceeding all expectations. Top speed was 441 mph, which was 50 mph faster than the Allison-powered version. Although the increased top speed was a bonus, other factors also came into play to make the Merlin-powered Mustang a great fighter. One of these was the ability to carry bombs or tanks under the wing, courtesy of the extra strengthening, whilst another few miles per hour of extra speed were gained by slight redesigning of the cowling in the area of the carburettor scoop.

As with all new aircraft, these first versions of the Mustang were to experience a few teething troubles, although these mainly concerned the engine production line. Initially the slowness of delivery meant that some completed aircraft were left standing around for up to six weeks awaiting a powerplant. Eventually Packard ironed out the glitches,

43-12102 is a unique airframe. Originally ordered as a P-51B, it was pulled from the manufacturing line to become the P-51D aerodynamic test vehicle. The cut-down rear fuselage and bubble canopy, which was to become the standard Mustang configuration, gave superb all-around visibility. (NAA Archive)

ensuring that engines would eventually be ready for installation as the aircraft moved down the production line. One major problem was to plague the Mustang throughout its long and distinguished service career, however. That was the effect of ground crew climbing off the wing over the leading edge rather than the trailing edge. Heavy military boots could dent or damage the perfectly shaped leading edge, which in flight caused some airflow distortion over the wing and a decrease in efficiency.

## Definitive Mustang

Following on from the P-51B/C Mustang came the much improved 'D' version. This had been evolved via the Malcolm-hooded Mustangs, aircraft whose sliding canopy included bulging to improve the pilot's area of vision. To further increase this advantage a single P-51B-1NA, airframe number 43-12102, was removed from the Inglewood production line for conversion. This involved reducing the rear fuselage decking and installing a tear-drop canopy.

The first flight of the modified aircraft was in September 1943, by pilot Bob Chilton. The pilot's area of vision was dramatically improved, although the change in shape resulted in a slight drop in overall top speed. This new version was designated the P-51D, and a total of 6,502 airframes were built at Inglewood plus a further 1,454 at the Dallas plant. These were designated as P-51K, which was essentially a slightly refined P-51D.

Other changes from 'B' to 'D' were far more subtle. These included simplification and lengthening of the cowlings, the installation of a Packard V-1650-7 engine rated at 1,695 hp, a standardised armament of six 0.50-inch Browning machine-guns and the permanent installation of an 85 gallon fuel tank in the rear fuselage. A slight problem with longitudinal stability was overcome later in the production run by the addition of a fin fillet, whilst the armament options were increased by fitting mountings for the very effective 5-inch High Velocity Aircraft Rockets (HVAR).

Further development of the Mustang saw the appearance of the two-seat trainer, which was designated the TP-51D. Other variants included the high-altitude XP-51F, a stripped version of the aircraft, whilst the follow-on XP-51G featured the Merlin RM145M rated at 1,500 hp which gave the lightweight Mustang incredible performance at altitude. The final experimental version of the lightweight fighter was the XP-51J, which was used as the test bed for the

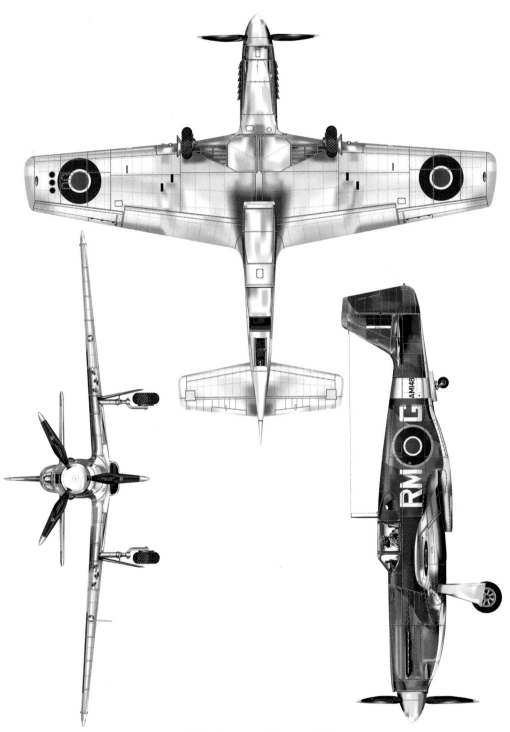

North American Mustang Mk I
No. 26 Squadron, RAF

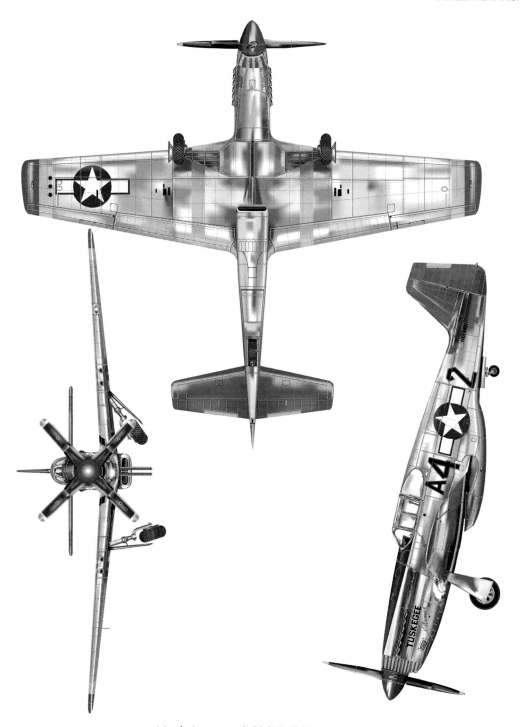

North American P-51C-5NT Mustang
Commemorative Air Force
In the colours of the 302nd Fighter Squadron, 332nd Fighter Group, 15th Air Force

Seen here on an early test flight, 44-83887 was the second XP-82 Twin Mustang prototype. Designed as a long-range fighter, the Twin Mustang saw service in Korea. Although a radical development of the Mustang, the P-82 nevertheless retains many of the design features which first appeared on the original NA-73X. *(NAA Archive)*

Allison V-1710-119 engine. This was intended as a standby powerplant should the licence to build the Packard Merlin lapse.

The final main production version of the Mustang was the P-51H, which benefited from the experience gained during the lightweight fighter programme. Powered by the Packard V-1650-7 with water injection, rated at 2,218 hp, this was the fastest Mustang of all with a top speed of 487 mph. Apart from the increase in power, changes were few, and mainly concentrated upon a simplified structure to which was added a taller fin for increased stability. Although hostilities had ceased by the time this variant entered service, a total of 555 were eventually constructed.

The final versions of the Mustang were radical departures from the original, most notably the P-82 fighter, which was essentially two lengthened P-51D fuselages joined by a new wing centre section.

## Post-war Mustangs

Although the Mustang was to leave regular USAF service soon after the end of the Korean War, there was a need for such a fighter in the air arms of many other less advanced air forces. To fill this gap, the Cavalier aircraft concern remanufactured and constructed new aircraft from spares, the most obvious difference in the resulting machines being a fin of increased height. The Mustang's final flourish was carried out by Piper. The company took over a project idea from Cavalier, proposing and flying turboprop versions of this famous aircraft. No production orders ensued.

# 2. Into the Wild Blue: Mustang in Service

The biggest user of the North American Mustang in all its forms was the USAAF and its post-war successor, the USAF. The first version to enter service was the A-36A Apache dive bomber, which paved the way for the fighter versions that followed. Although the USAAF took delivery of a number of Allison-powered P-51As, the type's time in the front line was short-lived once the more versatile Merlin-powered variants began to be delivered.

For the type to be truly effective it was needed in theatre in large quantities, which meant that many aircraft needed to be shipped at once. Mustangs manufactured at Inglewood were disassembled and placed into crates for shipment to Britain. The first unit destined to fly the type over Europe was the 354th Fighter Group (FG), which had originally trained to fly the Bell P-39 Airacobra. Men and machines travelled to their new home across the Atlantic in autumn 1943, with the crews arriving on 20 October. The Mustangs arrived soon after and were reassembled at RAF Greenham Common.

Once the unit was ready, it became part of the 9th Air Force, the USAAF's primary tactical command in Europe. Their operational base was Boxted, from which escort operations began almost immediately alongside the 354th and 363rd Fighter Squadrons (FS). Their initial missions included the protection of the bomber groups of the 8th Air Force, whose crews were suffering grievous losses at the hands of the *Luftwaffe* during their daylight bombing operations over Germany.

To give the Mustang increased range and loiter time over target, external tanks were developed for carriage on the underwing pylons. These would be jettisoned on the outward leg of a long-range sortie, or when engaging enemy fighters. The tanks were built in huge numbers, since the Mustangs got through hundreds on their missions, and production of these tanks peaked at 48,000 units in June 1944.

Other 9th AF operators of the NAA fighter included the 10th Photographic Group, which used the F-6 version for reconnaissance duties, and the combined 363rd Fighter/Tactical Reconnaissance Group (F/TRG), which combined both roles using the F-6D, the photo-reconnaissance version of the P-51D.

## Bomber Escort

The task of escorting the heavy bombers soon passed to the 8th AF itself, which had originally been forced to borrow aircraft from the 9th Air Force. P-51B/C and later P-51D models of the Mustang eventually replaced the original inventory of P-47 Thunderbolts, and quickly became masters of the skies over Germany. The 8th AF units that flew the Mustang included, in order of delivery, the 20th, 356th, 364th, 352nd, 359th, 4th, 355th, 361st, 479th, 78th, 339th, 353rd, 357th and the 55th Fighter Groups. Also using the Mustang were the 1st, 2nd and 3rd Support Flights.

Mustangs also saw combat service in a theatre that contrasted greatly with the skies over Europe. Operating with the 14th Air Force in China, Mustangs operated over the 'Hump' of the Himalayas, in support of bombing and supply missions. Many of the pilots were veterans from the Flying Tigers days, when the American Volunteer Group flew their Curtiss P-40s against the Japanese. To celebrate their heritage the Mustangs were painted with shark mouths on the engine cowlings. Initially assigned Allison P-51As and A-36As, they eventually standardised on the P-51D.

The Mustang's excellent range made it an ideal fighter for operations in the Pacific Theatre, where the P-51 served with the 5th Air Force. In December 1944 the pilots of the 3rd Air Commando Group began operations from the Philippines using the P-51D. In January 1945, the 348th FG exchanged its Thunderbolts for the P-51D, with the 35th FG following in March. The duty of reconnaissance was the remit of the 71st TRG, which replaced its Curtiss P-40s with the more capable F-6D and F-6K late in 1944. The role of the P-51 in the Pacific Zone was that of escort for the B-29 Superfortress bombers on their way to Japan, to provide defensive and anti-kamikaze fighter patrols, and to support ground troops directly engaging Japanese forces.

## Post-war service

Although the end of World War Two saw the cancellation of large Mustang production contracts, the career of this classic fighter was far from over. In the plans of the newly created United States Air Force, the P-51 became the F-51 and would become the prime equipment of the Air National Guard (ANG). The first unit to equip with the Mustang was the 120th Fighter Squadron of the Colorado Air National Guard, based at Buckley Field, Aurora, near Denver. In September 1946, the 110th Fighter Squadron of the Missouri ANG became the second Guard Mustang unit. Eventually most of the fighter squadrons of the ANG would fly the F-51, the 167th Fighter Interceptor Squadron of the West Virginia ANG finally disposing of its last aircraft in March 1957.

The ANG did experience a period when hanging on to its fighters was rather difficult. This situation had been triggered by the invasion of South Korea by the forces of Communist North Korea on 25 June 1950. Support quickly came from the USA, under the aegis of the United Nations. However, the USAF faced a serious problem. Its main operating bases were in Japan, and its primary fighter, the jet-powered Lockheed F-80, was very time-limited over the target as fuel consumption was high.

## Korean stopgap

There were available airfields in Korea, but these had been built by the Japanese for piston-powered fighters and were totally unsuitable for jet operations. The only other aircraft in theatre was the North American F-82 Twin Mustang, whose primary role was the defence of the Japanese islands. This aircraft was capable of reaching the desired targets, but was intended more for night-fighter and long-range interception duties.

Casting around for a more useful alternative the USAF settled upon the F-51 Mustang. There were thirty in store in Japan, whilst Major Dean Hess had another ten in South Korea where he was training pilots of the Republic of Korea Air Force in their operation. On 30 June a group of ROKAF pilots and their instructors moved to Taegu AB, close to the front line.

## Close support

Known as 'Bout One', the operations were a success from the outset, especially in the eyes of the Army's 24th Division, whose losses on numerous occasions were reduced due to the intervention of the Mustangs. This success prompted the area commander, Major General Frank Everest, to contact General Hoyt Vandenberg, the senior commander. On 3 July, he requested that as many F-51s as possible be despatched to Korea.

To meet the demand it was necessary to strip the ANG units of their aircraft. After much effort, a total of 145 aircraft were loaded aboard the carrier USS *Boxer* and despatched to Korea. Also aboard was a cadre of 70 experienced pilots who would join the war effort and reduce the workload on those personnel already in theatre.

As the *Boxer* and its cargo departed Alameda, Operation *Dallas* was in full swing. This saw the reactivation of the 30 mothballed aircraft in Japan, which were serviced and despatched to Korea and the airfield at Taegu, also known as

Showing evidence of hard usage, these four Mustangs are from the 357th FG. Originally assigned to the 9th AF, the group transferred to become the first P-51 group in the 8th AF in January 1944. All are of the high-backed P-51B/C variety, although only the lead aircraft has had a bulged Malcolm hood fitted for increased pilot visibility. It is clear from the strange slope that the last letter of the nearest fighter's identification markings was obviously applied whilst it was sitting on the ground. *(NAA Archive)*

Mustangs from the 18th Fighter-Bomber Wing (FBW) in Korea prepare to depart from K-4 past a dump containing the unit's supply of spare drop tanks. Pilots were requested to either return the drop tanks if possible or to release them behind allied lines for recovery later, hence the battered appearance of some of the tanks. *(USAF)*

After being retired from regular US Air Force use, the Mustang became a key part of the ANG's inventory. Airframe 44-64255 is an F-51H Mustang operated by the California ANG. Besides the obvious modifications to the airframe, this version, the fastest of the production Mustangs, also sports twin aerials on top of the fuselage whilst an Auto Direction Finding (ADF) loop is located under the canopy. *(C P Russell Smith Collection)*

K-2. To fly and maintain these aircraft, personnel were transferred from the 12th FS, part of the 18th FG based in the Philippines.

## Mustang build-up

By this time Operation *Bout One* had evolved into the 51st Provisional Fighter Squadron (PFS), part of the 5th AF. The first new aircraft into action came from those supplied under the *Dallas* operation, which began offensive missions on 15 July. Whilst the 5th PFS was building up its strength another unit was trading in its faster but less appropriate jet fighters for the Mustang. This was the 40th FS, whose experienced pilots began operations from Pohang AB (K-3) on 10 July. Not long after moving in, the squadron was called up to support an ROK regiment in serious trouble near the airbase. In appalling weather conditions the Mustangs flew mission after mission before the strong North Korean force was driven back.

Fortunately for the forces in Korea USS *Boxer* had arrived, and strenuous efforts were made to get its cargo of Mustangs ready for action. The first batch was despatched to the two units already in operation, whilst others were delivered to Taegu AB (K-2) to equip the 67th FS of the 18th Fighter-Bomber Group (FBG), which was declared ready for operations at the beginning of August. By this time the 51st PFS resumed its original designation as the 12th FBS. Further units were also beginning to convert from the F-80 Shooting Star to the earlier Mustang. One of the first was the 39th FS, which began operations from Pohang AB (K-3) on 7 August. This unit was followed by the entire 8th Fighter Group whose 35th FS began operations from Suwon (K-13) on 7 October whilst its sister unit the 36th FS flew from Kimpo AB (K-14).

Whilst the fighter versions were engaging in combat operations, one further airborne element was also re-equipping with the

Complete with wingtip fuel tanks, this F-51 Mustang is a Cavalier-converted aircraft which had started life as a standard P-51D. This aircraft and two more like it were used by the US Army as chase planes in high-speed helicopter trials. The finish was olive drab and white set off by a red fin tip. A similar colour was applied to the replacement wingtips when the tip tanks were removed. *(C P Russell Smith Collection)*

Mustang. On 3 September the 45th Tactical Reconnaissance Squadron (TRS) activated at Itazuke AB in Japan, where it would become part of the 67th Tactical Reconnaissance Wing (TRW). The squadron's original equipment consisted of the F-51 and RF-51 versions of the Mustang, and their role was that of both film and visual reconnaissance over the battlefield. Once declared ready the 45th TRS moved to Taegu AB with its F-51s in October, the RF-51s not arriving until the following month.

## Last service Mustangs

The Mustangs operating in Korea took a considerable beating, but they proved most effective in the roles assigned to them. However, the airfields on the Korean peninsula were being extended to allow jet operations, and the arrival of aircraft like the North American F-86 Sabre spelt the end of the Mustang's usage in Korea. The final mission flown by American F-51s was by the 67th FS on

23 January 1953. This was not the end for the Mustang in Korea, however, as units from other air forces continued to fly the type until the truce was finally signed later that year.

Although the Mustang was supposed to have disappeared from use with the United States armed forces by the end of the 1950s, it was to make one final appearance in the unlikely colours of the United States Army. The development of the Lockheed YAH-56A Cheyenne helicopter required the use of a fast, agile propeller-driven aircraft to act as a chase plane. Both the T-28 Trojan and a modified Beech U-21 Ute were used, although neither was really suitable for the role.

Further searching revealed that the USAF still had an airworthy F-51 available for chase plane duties, which the Army then borrowed. This machine, 0-72990, had been rebuilt by Cavalier Aircraft to extend its life and was exactly the right kind of aircraft for the task. One airframe was not enough, however, so the

Army ordered a further pair of aircraft from Cavalier. Both had started life as standard P-51Ds, but were extensively rebuilt before delivery in 1968.

The factors that made the Mustang ideal as a helicopter chase plane were its high top speed and excellent acceleration, both of which were needed to keep up with the YAH-56A. Their primary duties were recording on film the behaviour of the Cheyenne throughout each flight although a more active participation sometimes occurred during air combat simulation. All three aircraft were to eventually retire into preservation, including one to Fort Rucker in Alabama.

## First combat Mustangs

When the Mustang Mk I entered RAF service it was found to be inadequate in its performance above 11,000 feet, thanks to the limitations of its Allison engine. Having purchased the aircraft in quantity a role had to be found for it. Fortunately, the recently formed Army Co-operation Command had a niche for the new machine. Intended as a link between ground and air forces, the command provided an early form of Forward Air Control (FAC).

The first unit to equip with the Mustang Mk I was No. 26 Sqn, although it was very lightly employed as the opportunities to support ground troops in Europe had disappeared after the evacuation of Dunkirk. Whilst the Army regrouped, retrained and prepared to resume the fight, the aircraft of No. 26 Sqn found other employment. This took the form of armed reconnaissance missions over occupied Europe, which the squadron's aircraft flew in pairs. One of the fighters had a single F.24 camera situated behind the pilot's seat on the port side whilst the other flew armed support and interference.

## High-speed reconnaissance

Each mission was flown at high speed and low level, with the reconnaissance machine covering the required installations whilst the other watched for fighters. Both, however, were vulnerable to the deadly anti-aircraft fire sent up by the defending *Luftwaffe* units. The first sorties, which began on 10 May 1942, had originally been flown by singleton aircraft

under the title of Operation *Popular*. This name continued when they started flying in pairs. Unfortunately, this sort of low-level operation is risky, and losses were inevitable. The first combat loss came on 14 July, when a Mustang flew into the ground on a strafing run.

The dangers of low flying were compensated for by the fact that the Mustang could more than hold its own at low level, as Flying Officer Hollis of No. 414 (Canadian) Sqn showed when he shot down an Fw 190 that was harassing his wingman. Other Mustang Mk Is were employed on 'Rhubarbs', as the RAF's high-speed, low-level search-and-destroy missions carried out over Europe were called.

The RAF operated altogether more than 600 Mustang Mk I, Mk IA and P-51As in the four years to the end of hostilities in 1945, with fewer than 100 surviving in use at the end of the war. Overall the RAF formed sixteen of the planned eighteen squadrons for Army Co-operation use. There was one other unit that flew the Allison Mustang. No. 516 Sqn was assigned to support combined operations, but even today few of its classified missions have been revealed.

## Anglo-American hybrid

The first Merlin-powered version of the Mustang to be flown by the RAF was the Mustang Mk III, which was equivalent to the P-51B/C. Early deliveries had the original flat-sided cockpit, but most later aircraft had the bulged cockpit canopy known as the Malcolm hood. The first unit to receive the Mustang III was No. 19 Sqn in February 1944. Based at Ford in Sussex, its duties included escorting tactical bombers on raids to France before the Normandy invasion of that summer. Other units flying the type spent their time knocking down V-1 flying bombs, and in North Africa, the Mediterranean and Italy the Mk III replaced aging Kittyhawks and Hurricanes in the inventory of the Desert Air Force.

Some 900 Mustang Mk IVs and IVAs were delivered to the RAF. Equivalent to the American P-51Ds and Ks, these aircraft equipped squadrons within Fighter Command, and also served with the Germany-based 2nd Allied Tactical Air Force (ATAF) at the end of the war. Overall the Mustang equipped

A Mustang Mk I undergoes field maintenance and refuelling. The XC code indicates No. 26 Squadron RAF, the world's first operational Mustang unit, which entered combat in May 1942. *(C P Russell Smith Collection)*

Carrying hastily applied D-Day stripes, this Malcolm-hooded Mustang Mk III is seen at around the time of the invasion of Normandy in June 1944. FB226 was assigned to No. 122 Sqn. *(C P Russell Smith Collection)*

Wearing the 'DV' codes of No. 129 Sqn, Mustang Mk IV KH727 begins a sortie in 1945. The dark banding on the fin is a small segment of camouflage which remained behind the fin flash. *(C P Russell Smith Collection)*

eighteen Fighter Command and two ATAF squadrons, with a further five flying the type in the Mediterranean theatre. The last RAF Mustang mission, flown by Fighter Command, took place in November 1946.

## Commonwealth Mustangs

Given its excellent performance, it is not surprising that the Mustang was very popular with other air forces. British Commonwealth air forces were some of the first to receive the P-51, when they replaced less effective aircraft or supplemented the current inventory. One of the first recipients, the Royal Australian Air Force, received aircraft direct from the American production line as well as from the local Commonwealth Aircraft Corporation (CAC) production line at Fisherman's Bend.

Eventually 100 Mustangs were delivered to the RAAF, where they fully or partially equipped eight squadrons. Fully equipped units included Nos. 21, 22, 23 and 25 Sqns of the Citizens' Air Force, plus Nos. 75, 76 and 77 Sqns of the full-time RAAF. The latter unit served alongside USAF forces in Korea, being based at Pohang, Yonpo and Pusan air bases during 1950. The only other unit to use the Mustang in front-line service was No. 3 Sqn, which flew the fighter alongside locally built Wirraway and Auster III aircraft on tactical reconnaissance missions.

New Zealand was also an operator of the P-51. In 1945 the dominion ordered 370 aircraft, an initial batch of 30 P-51D-25NTs to be followed by P-51Ms. As the war in the Pacific ended before delivery, New Zealand cancelled the greater part of the order, but had to accept the 30 airframes already *en route*. They were placed in storage until a decision could be made about their employment.

In 1951 they were brought out of storage to equip four squadrons of the Territorial Air Force, with No. 4 Sqn being the first to become operational. The Mustangs did not serve long, however, as they were withdrawn in August 1955. This was nominally due to corrosion and undercarriage problems, although some sources suggest that pilots were having trouble landing these high-performance machines.

Half a world away, the Royal Canadian Air Force was receiving its second tranche of

Mustangs, having operated the Mustang Mk I as part of the RAF during the war. This second run of aircraft comprised P-51Ds. A total of 100 were ordered late in 1945, and went on to equip front-line squadrons, the selected units being Nos. 400, 401, 402, 424, 438 and 442. P-51s were also used by support units and training squadrons. After their replacement by jet fighters, the Mustangs were passed on to organisations like No. 102 Composite Unit, where they were used for support duties, which included target towing.

## South Africa

South Africa began using the Mustang from 24 September 1944, when No. 5 Sqn replaced its obsolete P-40 Kittyhawks with P-51B/Cs. These early Mustangs were in turn replaced by P-51Ds and P-51Ks. No. 5 Sqn SAAF disbanded in October 1945, but this was not the end of the Mustang in SAAF service. The South Africans sent a contingent to take part in the United Nations defence of Korea, a force including a fighter squadron that would fly Mustangs for much of the war. No. 2 'Cheetah' Sqn SAAF became part of the 18th FBW based at Pusan (K-9), and began operations on 19 November 1950. These would continue until 1953, when the F-86 Sabre replaced the Mustangs. During their period in action, the squadron flew a total of 10,737 sorties, during which 12 pilots were killed in action whilst another 30 were captured or posted as missing. 74 aircraft of the 95 operated were lost in combat.

## P-51 in Europe

The Mustang also proved to be a popular mount for European fighter squadrons. One of the first countries to use the type was France. Initial deliveries to the *Armee de l'Air* began in late 1944, with operations beginning over Germany early in 1945. The first Mustang unit was GC II/33, a tactical reconnaissance squadron, which was equipped with both the F-6C and F-6D, the reconnaissance equivalents of the P-51C and the P-51D respectively. The F-6 remained in use until the mid 1950s.

Italy was also a major post-war Mustang operator, receiving the first of its 173 aircraft in September 1947 under the auspices of the Military Assistance Program (MAP). Soon after

Wearing the 'CB' codes of the Central Flying School, this Royal Canadian Air Force Mustang is fully equipped with underwing mounting points, though the wing gun armament is blocked off. As with many post-war Mustangs, this aircraft has an ADF loop located under the canopy. (C P Russell Smith Collection)

Flown by No. 3 Sqn of the RNZAF, NZ2403 carries the unit's orange and black check bars. It was one of thirty Mustangs delivered to New Zealand at the end of World War Two. (C P Russell Smith Collection)

In 1950 the South African Air Force sent F-51s to Korea as part of the United Nations force. They were flown by No. 2 Sqn alongside their USAF counterparts, as part of the 18th FBW. (USAF)

First equipping with Mustangs at the end of 1944, the French *Armee de l'Air* would continue to fly later models of the type on reconnaissance duties into the 1950s, until they were replaced by jets. The three F-6Ds seen here in formation belong to GC II/33. By the time this photo was taken, in the late 1940s, the earlier F-6C conversions of the P-51B had been retired. *(C P Russell Smith Collection)*

In the service of the Royal Swedish Air Force the Mustang was referred to as the J26. The primary operating unit was F16, normally based at Uppsala. Evidence of its previous ownership is discernible on the fuselage. Most Swedish Mustangs had been sold to Latin America by 1954. (C P Russell Smith Collection)

arrival, the first specimens underwent extensive testing before being issued to front-line squadrons, which included Nos. 3, 4, 5, 6 and 51 *Stormo*. No. 4 *Stormo* also flew a handful of Mustangs in the target-towing role. The F-51 finally left Italian service in 1958. This was not the complete end of the Italian Mustangs, however, as a quantity were transferred to the Somali Air Force, where they remained in service until the arrival of Soviet-built aircraft in the 1960s.

## Interned and flown

The Mustang was first seen in Swedish skies during World War Two, when USAAF pilots in damaged aircraft flew to neutral Sweden to avoid captivity in Germany. The aircraft were interned, and the Royal Swedish Air Force, or *Flygvapnet*, began to operate them under the local designation of J26. Most were P-51Bs or Cs. Even before the end of the war, Sweden ordered a further 50 P-51Ds, also designated J26, which entered service with F16 at Uppsala. Further machines, more than ninety in total, were supplied at the end of hostilities. The first aircraft entered service in 1945, with the last of the 157 machines delivered arriving in March 1948. Whilst in use a dozen of these aircraft

were converted to S26 standard for photo-reconnaissance work.

With the arrival of the Vampire and J29 jet fighters, the days of Sweden's Mustangs were numbered. Their disposal was mainly to other countries – 25 went to Israel, 26 to Nicaragua, and 41 to the Dominican Republic, these sales taking place between 1952–4.

## Messerschmitt replacement

Neutral Switzerland also acquired Mustangs through internment during the war. After the war a new fighter was needed to replace the Messerschmitt Bf 109s acquired from Nazi Germany. The chosen aircraft was the P-51D of which 100 were ordered with deliveries beginning in 1948. Their tenure was intended to be short, as the de Havilland Vampire was required as the primary fighter type. However, delays in Vampire production meant that they remained in front-line service until 1956 when the greater majority were scrapped.

The final European nation to fly the Mustang was the Netherlands, which received forty P-51Ds for operations in the Dutch East Indies. Deliveries began to Nos. 121 and 122 Sqns just before VJ day. Initially they were used in support of ground troops fighting against

A rare photo of a P-51B in Nationalist Chinese markings moving down the North American line at Inglewood. Also visible are aircraft destined for the RAF and the USAAF. In the late 1940s, the Chinese Communists made use of captured Nationalist Mustangs until the arrival of Soviet aircraft. *(NAA Archive)*

An F-51D Mustang of the Republic of Korea Air Force. Rocket pylons flank the main ordnance/fuel pylon next to the undercarriage. Also worthy of note is the auxiliary vent door at the base of the radiator fairing – a feature which, when opened in flight, gave the fighter extra thrust. *(C P Russell Smith Collection)*

Indonesian freedom fighters. When the Dutch pulled out in 1951, and the Netherlands East Indies Air Force was disbanded, the remaining Mustangs formed the core of the emergent Indonesian Air Force. They remained in service with the *Angkatan Udara Republik Indonesia* until replaced by Soviet jet fighters in 1959.

In the Far East, the Chinese Nationalist Air Force operated a variety of Mustangs including the P-51B/C and P-51D versions. These

Sitting on the ramp at Clark AFB, this F-51D was assigned to the 6th FBW of the Philippine Air Force. Airframe 44-73622 was second-hand; it had been flown by the USAF before transfer. With more than 160 aircraft delivered, the PAF was one of the largest users of Mustangs through the 1950s. Most were withdrawn from service at the end of the decade following a series of accidents. *(C P Russell Smith Collection)*

eventually were moved to Taiwan in 1949 following the Communist triumph on the mainland. Some captured examples were used briefly by the Communist forces, though spares and maintenance were problems. Eventually they were replaced by Soviet aircraft.

## Mustangs in Asia

Another country that used the Mustang against Communist forces was, of course, South Korea. Its first P-51Ds arrived in 1950, the pilots being trained under the aegis of Major Dean Hess. These fighters remained the mainstay of the ROKAF until 1960, when the North American F-86 came into use.

The Philippine Air Force came into existence in 1947 when the islands gained independence from the United States. An initial batch of nearly forty aircraft was originally transferred, rather reluctantly, from USAF stocks to the emergent PAF. Eventually an estimated total of 160 aircraft was delivered. In PAF service the Mustangs were operated by the 5th, 6th and 8th

Fighter Wings and the training school. The local aerobatic team, 'The Blue Diamonds', also flew the P-51s. A first display was flown in early 1953 and the team continued in existence until the end of 1954.

The end for the Mustang in Philippine service came in 1959, when one crash too many occurred. After thirty such incidents, PAF Headquarters decided that the Mustangs should be disposed of, and the final flight took place at the end of June 1959.

## In service with Israel

The only Middle Eastern operator of the Mustang was Israel. At least two aircraft had turned up in the newly created state just prior to the War of Independence during 1948–9. Serving with No. 101 Sqn these two machines flew scores of sorties and succeeded in shooting down at least one enemy aircraft. Even though an arms embargo was placed upon the country, by various clandestine means, Israel managed to acquire a further twenty-five Mustangs,

Photographs of counter-insurgency Mustangs of the *Fuerza Aerea Guatemala* in their early unpainted form are extremely rare. The number 348 appears faintly on the nose of this P-51, which also sports gloss dark blue wingtips and spinner as its flight colours. (*Tulio Soto Collection*)

most being ex-Swedish aircraft. The P-51Ds remained in front-line service alongside the Supermarine Spitfire until finally replaced by jets in the 1950s.

## Latin-American Mustangs

Far and away the biggest market for reworked or surplus Mustangs, at least in the type's later years, was in Latin America, or more particularly in Central America.

Costa Rica is located in the narrow strip of land that connects North and South America. Very much under the care of the United States, the *Fuerza Aerea Costarricense* gained four P-51D Mustangs by the simple expedient of a direct transfer from the Texas ANG in 1955. They were serialled 1 to 4, and the survivor (No. 4) was sold to an American collector in 1964. Surprisingly, Cuba was also home for three civilianised Mustangs that were acquired by nefarious means during 1959. They served with the *Fuerza Aerea Revolucionaria* until replaced by Soviet aircraft in the 1960s.

## Counter-insurgency

The Central American nation of Guatemala had a struggle to acquire the North American

P-51D. Twice, in 1951 and 1953, the United States rebuffed approaches from President Arevalo and his successor, President Arbenz. At the time, the height of the McCarthy witch hunts, the State Department regarded the administrations of both as Communist sympathisers. The Arbenz government then attempted to purchase some of the surplus ex-Swedish machines, though this move too was successfully blocked by the United States. However, just over the border, the CIA was supporting an armed insurrection led by Castillo Armas. The Americans supplied a pair of P-51Ds and three P-47 Thunderbolts to the rebels, and when battle was finally joined these five aircraft were to tip the balance in favour of the insurrectionists who successfully brought down the Arbenz regime.

Once order had been restored to US satisfaction, a further three Mustangs were supplied to the *Fuerza Aerea Guatemala* on 20 December 1954. Two further batches of three and seven respectively were later supplied, as was a single TF-51D which brought the total supplied to the FAG to sixteen aircraft. A further increase in the strength of the *Escuadron Costa Atlantico* occurred in 1957 when fourteen

Once the property of the Swedish Air Force, this Mustang was later transferred to the *Fuerza Aerea Dominicana* as 1923. Operated as front-line aircraft for many years, the Mustangs were eventually sold at a good profit to collectors. The profits helped fund the purchase of Cessna A-37s for the FAD. *(C P Russell Smith Collection)*

former Royal Canadian Air Force machines were supplied. Officially, thirty Mustangs were supplied, although it is rumoured that some ex-Israeli machines were also acquired. Whilst in service the F-51Ds were employed on counter-insurgency work against local guerrilla forces, though time was also found to create an aerobatic team known as the 'Quetzales'. The existence of this team came to an end in January 1972 when three of the team collided. Withdrawal from use came soon afterwards, the surviving aircraft being sold (at a profit) to rich American collectors.

South of Guatemala is Nicaragua, whose history is littered with governmental changes of a violent nature. In 1947, the signing of the Rio Pact allowed the Nicaraguan air force to update its equipment. Part of the new inventory was a batch of ex-Swedish Mustangs. Totalling 26 in all, they were delivered in 1950 with a further dozen being made available from USAF stocks in 1954. Another eight Mustangs were obtained from various unidentified sources in the 1950s. The operating unit was the *Fuerza Aerea de la Guardia Nacional de Nicaragua*, or the Nicaraguan National Guard Air Force. The F-51 unit remained in

existence until 1972, when the aircraft were disposed of.

## The Football War

Also located in Central America is the Republic of El Salvador, whose entry into the ranks of Mustang ownership came very late. It did not occur until the early 1960s, when a total of fourteen were delivered including one TF-51D. One final delivery of five remanufactured aircraft was undertaken in 1968. The whole force became engaged in the infamous 'Football War' against Honduras, which erupted after the score of the World Cup qualifier match was disputed. During the fighting, five Mustangs were lost, two to a mid-air collision, two because of fuel starvation and one was shot down. The final survivors, which included machines purchased after the fighting, were eventually retired in 1974.

## Caribbean Mustangs

The *Fuerza Aerea Dominicana* purchased thirty-two ex-Swedish F-51D Mustangs in 1952 to equip an *Escuadron de Caza* which became operational in October of that year. More were acquired over the years, including ten supplied

One of the beneficiaries of American largesse when it came to armaments was the *Fuerza Aerea Uruguaya*, whose *Grupo Aviacion* No. 2 would eventually operate No. 262 after delivery. Replaced by Lockheed Shooting Stars in 1960, the Mustangs were sold to Bolivia, with the survivors finally being retired in 1977. *(Tulio Soto Collection)*

after refurbishment by Cavalier Aircraft. The Mustangs saw limited combat service during an uprising in 1965; at least one was lost. Having operated more than sixty-seven Mustangs in thirty years, the end for Dominican F-51s came in 1984 when the last few were sold to collectors for $300,000 each.

## 'Toothless' operations

The Haitian Air Corps gained its first combat aircraft in the early 1950s, when six ex-USAF Mustangs were delivered and began operating from Bowen Field, close to Port-au-Prince. However, the wing-mounted armament was kept in the presidential armoury as dictator 'Papa Doc' Duvalier was paranoid about the possibility of revolution. Although the aircraft remained in use through the 1960s, mercenaries replaced local pilots. Surviving aircraft were updated by Cavalier and remained in use until final withdrawal in October 1973.

One of the few countries in South America proper which operated the P-51 was Uruguay.

In 1947 an American air mission arrived in the country to reorganise the air force. Amongst the aircraft delivered were twenty-five Mustangs, which formed the inventory of *Grupo de Aviacion* No. 2 from 1950. They were to remain in service until 1960, when they were retired in favour of the Lockheed F-80C jet fighter, some eight survivors passing to Bolivia.

The *Fuerza Aerea Boliviano* received its first four aircraft from Uruguay in 1960. Another batch of four entered service in 1968. To reinforce the FAB, Project *Peace Condor* was initiated, which funded the supply of eight Cavalier-rebuilt F-51Ds. These were delivered in 1968 although only four were fully to Cavalier conversion standards. The operating units of these venerable fighters were the *Grupo Aereo* No. 2 based at Colcapirua and the *Grupo Aereo de Caza* based at Santa Cruz. Whilst in service at least one F-51D was lost in an accident on 30 July 1970. The Mustang finally left FAB service during 1977, being replaced by the Lockheed/Canadair T-33.

# 3. Creating the Legend: Mustang People

For all of the human qualities ascribed to it by enthusiasts, the North American P-51 Mustang and its various offshoots are no more than machines. Tools, with as much practical purpose and, to some, as little romance as a tractor. But it is undeniably true that the Mustang has come to symbolise something more – in part, the combination of graceful lines and power, and in part, its enviable combat record. Above all, like a very few classic combat aircraft, the Mustang has come to represent the people who were and are associated with it. This not only includes the pilots who took it into combat and forged the public face of the Mustang, but the backroom boys who designed, built and maintained it. To their numbers must be added modern restorers of this famous fighter, whose efforts enthral the crowds wherever they fly, from local air shows to the world-famous Reno Air Races.

## 'Father' of the Mustang

Top of the heap must come the man responsible for building up the North American Aviation company, James H 'Dutch' Kindelberger. As President of NAA, Kindelberger, in company with his management team, persuaded the British to order the new fighter, and later persuaded the USAAF to accept the Mustang as the A-36A Apache dive bomber. To secure potential orders from the British Purchasing Commission, Kindelberger and his team briefed Sir Henry Self and the rest of the BPC on the proposed design of the NA-73X. Also present on that day were the NAA Vice-President Lee Atwood, Chief Engineer Ray Rice and the head of the design team, Edgar Schmued, who has frequently been called the father of the Mustang. Some credit must also be due to the British, who ordered the NA-73X instead of the previously requested Curtiss Kittyhawk fighters, a known if less-than-ideal quantity, rather than the step into the unknown, which the Mustang represented.

Another specialist who was to join the team later was aerodynamicist Edward Horkey, whose main claim to fame is that he developed the laminar-flow wing, which was only partly based on data from NACA. Further unexpected propulsive advances were to be made by the same team when it was discovered that opening the flap at the rear of the radiator housing actually created thrust: acting as a primitive ram-jet, the expelled air increased the Mustang's top speed by several knots.

Test pilots also played an important part in the development of the Mustang. Some touched the programme only briefly, while others were lucky enough to stay for the duration. The short-term stayers included the flamboyant Vance Breese, who undertook the maiden and early test-flights of the prototype. He was followed by the unfortunate Paul Balfour, who crashed the NA-73X on his first flight. Balfour's replacement was RC 'Bob' Chilton, who would go on to fly all the development machines as well as undertaking the pre-delivery test flights of hundreds of production aircraft. Eventually this doyen of Mustang test-flying would achieve more than 3,000 hours on the type. To achieve such a total Bob Chilton would sometimes make up to ten flights per day on production aircraft, although his self-confessed favourites were the experimental lightweight fighters.

Having progressed beyond the development and acceptance stage, the first Mustangs into combat were the Mk Is of the Royal Air Force. Although these first examples of the breed had performance problems at altitude, the Allison Mustang's fine low-level ability meant that it could more than hold its own in the right circumstances. The Mustang's first victory – the first of thousands – came soon after the Mk I entered service. The location was Dieppe and the date was 19 August 1942. American-born, Canadian-trained and serving with the RAF, Pilot Officer Hollis H Hills successfully downed a Focke-Wulf Fw 190. This most unique of pilots eventually returned to serve in the American forces, specifically the US Navy, where he continued his combat scoring run. Other Mustang victories during this period included three claimed by Douglas 'Bitsy' Grant, and on another occasion a pair of Mustang Mk Is successfully downed five enemy fighters during one engagement.

## Apache ace

Whilst the Allison-engined Mustangs of the RAF were beginning make a name for themselves over France and the Low Countries, their dive-bomber equivalents were also starting to assert themselves. Although the least-known version of the Mustang, the A-36A Apache was more than capable of scoring aerial victories. The A-36A began its operational career with the 27th Fighter-Bomber Group based at Ras el Ma in French Morocco. One of the first missions was the mass aerial assault upon the island of Pantelleria, the effect of which was the surrender of the occupying Axis forces. Both the 27th FBG and the other A-36A operating unit, the 311th FBG, moved onto the island airfield, from which the campaign to free Sicily would begin. During this intense period of fighting Lieutenant Michael T Russo of the 27th FBG would become the only ace in the Apache, although his colleagues within both groups would push the total of confirmed kills up to 84 enemy aircraft for the campaign.

As the USAAF was the greatest user of the Mustang in all its forms it is hardly surprising that this organisation created the most aces. One of the first was the exceptionally self-effacing Captain Don 'Gentle' Gentile, a fighter pilot assigned to the 4th Fighter Group, 8th Air Force based at Debden in Essex. On the ground Don Gentile was a quiet, shy and slightly nervous man, but put him in a cockpit and the transformation was incredible. Gone were the self-conscious traits and in their place came a supremely confident fighter pilot who exhibited all the attributes needed for such a job – flying skill, superb vision, fast reflexes and outstanding judgement. After one medal presentation ceremony presided over by General Dwight D Eisenhower the comment was made that Captain Gentile, now the holder of the Distinguished Service Cross, was a one-man air force.

## Mustang maestro

Born in December 1920 in the state of Ohio, Don Gentile got the aviation bug at an early age, applying to join the US Army Air Corps as soon as he was able. Although considered to have potential, he was told to go away and improve his education, a process that seemed pointless to a youngster who just wanted to fly.

The fall of France was to change Don Gentile's life. The RAF was desperate for pilots, and he was quickly signed up by the RAF recruiting office in Cleveland, Ohio. A period under training in Canada was followed by a transatlantic voyage and commissioning as a Pilot Officer on 11 November 1941. Assigned to the Spitfire-equipped No. 133 Sqn, his first, uneventful mission was on 22 June 1942 as wingman to Flight Lieutenant Cobly King. A further sortie in support of RAF Bostons attacking the Abbeville base of the *Luftwaffe*'s JG 26 soon changed his perspective. Although the bombing raid was a success the journey home was anything but. From out of almost nowhere a flight of Fw 190s jumped the escorting fighters, quickly shooting several down. Good instincts and desperate evasive flying were to save Don Gentile on that day.

On 19 August Don Gentile scored his first two victories. Three days later he was a member of the USAAF, as the RAF's American

One of the first and greatest of Mustang aces, former Eagle Squadron pilot Don S Gentile flew P-51B 'Shangri-La' in the early months of 1944, running his score up to 21 confirmed kills before returning to the USA. Gentile usually flew with with fellow ace John T Godfrey (18 kills) in the 336th FS, 4th FG, based at Debden in Essex. The aircraft was written off when Gentile crash-landed after buzzing the airfield in April 1944. *(USAF)*

squadrons – Nos. 71, 121 and 133 – were transferred into the 4th FG becoming the 334th, 335th and 336th Fighter Squadrons. The 4th FG, nicknamed 'Blakeslee's Bachelors' after its commander, Colonel Don Blakeslee, were to become the highest-scoring combat group in the European Theatre of Operations.

## The 'Deadly Duo'

After more than a year on the P-47 Thunderbolt, the Group re-equipped with the P-51 in February 1944. Early in March, the group undertook a bomber escort mission to Berlin during which the deteriorating weather saw the fighters separated from the bombers. On the way home the Mustangs became entangled with a group of Bf 109s and Fw 190s. In the ensuing mêlée Don Gentile shot down a pair of Focke-Wulfs, whilst his regular wingman John T Godfrey damaged another. Five days later, on 8 March 1944, another mission over Berlin saw the pair shooting down six enemy fighters between them.

Further sorties during that month saw Don Gentile rack up nine enemy aircraft confirmed whilst his overall total had risen to twenty-one. Gentile's and Godfrey's Mustangs carried the standard red noses of the 4th Fighter Group, but they they also sported red and white checks under the exhaust stacks so that they could recognise each other in the air. The final mission flown by Don Gentile was undertaken on 13 April. This mission was not one of his best, as, in a fit of high spirits he buzzed the airfield at Debden. Misjudging his approach he had to crash-land his Mustang in front of waiting reporters.

Fortunately, he survived this mishap and returned to the United States to take part in a Bond selling tour. Having survived the hazards of a long war it was the final irony that a pilot as skilful as Don Gentile would be killed saving the life of a fellow serviceman whilst flying a Lockheed T-33 on a training sortie.

## 4th Fighter Group

As the 4th Fighter Group was one of the most successful units in the ETO it is not surprising that they would produce more aces than other groups. Major Pierce 'Mac' McKennon was already a successful fighter pilot when he came

to the 4th FG. He thoroughly enjoyed the transition to the P-51 Mustang, which was far more manoeuvrable and lighter than the mighty Thunderbolt he had been flying, as well as being faster and longer-ranged than the Spitfire he had flown with the RAF.

His first mission in a Mustang in March 1944 saw Mac shoot down a Bf 109, which made him an ace. Further victories followed over the next month, during which McKennon practised his other art of piano playing in the Officer's Club, which made him a 'one-man morale section'. By the end of May, at the end of his tour of duty, he had been credited with ten victories.

After a period of rest and recuperation in the United States, Mac returned to combat flying in August 1944 when he rejoined the 4th FG as commander of the 335th Fighter Squadron at Debden. By now equipped with the P-51D, McKennon found that the *Luftwaffe* was much less evident, and most missions were ground-attack in nature.

This was not without hazard as Mac found out to his cost whilst attacking a troop train. Such was the intensity of the defending flak that the Mustang was damaged and could not continue. Major McKennon bailed out and managed to avoid capture, eventually returning home to Debden in September 1944.

## Amazing rescue

Mac McKennon was then to play a part in one of the most daring rescue missions undertaken during World War Two. Whilst leading his squadron on a long-range escort mission to Berlin, his Mustang, 'Ridge Runner', was hit by flak. Taking to the silk to escape his burning aircraft, McKennon landed safely, but being hundreds of miles into enemy territory he was resigned to being captured. However, his circling red-nosed compatriots had other ideas. Lieutenant George Green came down low, made three passes over the field in which his CO was standing, then dropped flaps and undercarriage before touching down in front of his startled boss. Seeing rescue up close, Mac climbed aboard the Mustang. Some place-swapping went on as George Green sat on his CO's lap to make the most difficult take-off of his career and to set course for home. With the rest of the group's aircraft clustered around the

This P-51D is being flown by Lt Urban L Drew of the 361st FG over France in the summer of 1944. Drew would have been remembered, if at all, as a fairly representative Mustang pilot, were it not for his feat on 7 October 1944. On a mission over Germany, Drew spotted two Messerschmitt Me 262s taking off from Achmer. Attacking while the jets were still slow and vulnerable, he destroyed both within seconds of each other. *(USAF)*

rescue aircraft, the whole formation set course westwards for Debden, which was safely reached some three hours later.

## P-47 and P-51 Ace

Duane W Beeson was born in 1921 at Boise, Idaho. He enlisted in the Royal Canadian Air Force in 1941, and was posted to No. 71 'Eagle' Sqn, later transferring to the 334th FS, part of the 4th FG. Nicknamed 'Bee', he named his aircraft 'Boise Bee'. Beeson was one of the few 4th FG pilots to achieve real success in the P-47, scoring more than 12 victories in the Thunderbolt. He was to be promoted to CO of

the 334th FS in March 1944. By this time the unit had traded in its Thunderbolts for Mustangs and he would score his remaining kills in a P-51.

Duane Beeson was a consistent fighter pilot, scoring single or even double victories many times. From 18 May 1943 to 5 April 1944, Major Beeson shot down German aircraft on fifteen different occasions, scoring most heavily in early 1944 over Germany itself. All but one of his kills were against single-engined fighters.

On 5 April 1944 the fighter group was strafing airfields near Berlin. After one successful attack which had left many burning

Junkers Ju 88s on the ground, the Mustangs spotted another field with five Ju 88s parked wingtip to wingtip along the perimeter track. Diving into the attack, the Americans saw the first burst into flame and strikes all over the others as well as an Me 323 transport. Just as Beeson opened fire, tracers flashed past the cockpit and the Mustang was hit. Leaving the airfield behind, he climbed the badly damaged aircraft to 1,000 feet and tried to get the engine restarted again but so much coolant had been lost that he had to bail out. By the time he got free of the cockpit, available altitude had dropped to 400 feet. Fortunately for Duane Beeson his parachute opened just in time to save his life. He spent the next thirteen months as a POW, having scored twenty-four air-to-air victories and a further four on the ground.

Although the 4th FG was very much an 8th AF success story it was by no means the only group to produce a crop of aces. Captain Clarence Emil 'Bud' Anderson flew 116 sorties with the 362nd FS of the 357th FG, claiming 16.25 victories in the process, becoming the fourth-ranking ace of that outstanding group. A native of Newcastle, California, Anderson had been working at the Sacramento Air Depot when the Japanese attacked Pearl Harbor. Within the month he had enlisted in the Army Air Corps and left for the war. He did his primary training at Lindbergh Field, San Diego, going on to advanced training at Luke Field near Phoenix, Arizona. After progressing through various training units Bud Anderson joined the 357th FG which had originally been equipped with P-39 Airacobras.

Complete with owner Peter McManus's name on the canopy frame, this P-51D is painted to represent that flown by John Meyer, one of the highest-scoring aces of the 8th AF, with 24 confirmed victories (23 individual kills and two shared). Meyer's original Mustang, nicknamed 'Petie', was shot down with another pilot at the controls on D-Day. Meyer scored 15 kills in its successor, 'Petie 2nd'. (Nicholas A Veronico)

Flying in formation are P-51Ds 'Straw Boss II' and 'Ridge Runner III'. The former was originally built as 44-72192 whilst the latter is painted to represent the aircraft flown by 8th AF ace Major Pierce 'Mac' McKennon. McKennon was shot down by flak while strafing Prenzlau airfield in March 1945, but he was rescued by Lt George Green, who landed his P-51 and picked up his 4th FG squadron-mate. *(Nicholas A Veronico)*

However, the group was re-equipped with the P-51 Mustang and moved to its base at Leiston in Britain, from which Anderson undertook his first mission on 8 January 1944. On 3 March 1944 his first victory was against a Messerschmitt Bf 109 which had been attacking a straggling B-17 on one of the first escorted Berlin missions. On 29 June 1944 Anderson shot down his first Fw 190 while escorting a bomber raid over Leipzig. It was one of three kills he claimed for that mission.

Anderson stayed with the USAF after the war and for many years served as a test pilot. He spent a lot of time on a project that, in retrospect, seems a little adventurous. This involved the use of parasite fighters attached to a bomber's wingtip to provide defence over the target. He also flew F-105 Thunderchiefs in Vietnam, and retired from the Air Force as a full Colonel. During a 1995 Warbirds air show, on the 50th anniversary of their last combat mission together, he and his great friend Chuck Yeager got back into a Mustang, and flew over the show. Bud did a victory roll over the airstrip to celebrate the occasion.

## The 'Right Stuff'

One of America's greatest pilots, General Chuck Yeager's accomplishments as a fighter ace have been overshadowed by his later achievements as a test pilot, but his fighter pilot experiences were remarkable in their own right. An eighteen-year-old West Virginia country boy, he joined the USAAF in 1941. By the age of twenty-two, he would have shot down eleven and a half German aircraft, including two Me 262 jets. He would also be shot down over France, evade the Germans, join the French Maquis resistance fighters and make his way back to England via the Spanish escape route.

Charles 'Chuck' Yeager graduated from Hamlin High School in 1941, and became an aircraft mechanic. He originally loathed flying, having been violently ill after his first time in the air. But when the chance came to become a 'Flying Sergeant', with three stripes and no onerous duties, he applied, and was accepted for flying training. His natural aptitude allied to good co-ordination, mechanical abilities, and excellent memory impressed his instructors. Once qualified, Yeager was assigned to the

357th FG, which was undergoing training on the P-39 for escort duties over Europe. Before they got into action, however, the Bell fighters had been replaced by the P-51.

The 357th FG moved to Europe at the end of 1943. It began operations in February 1944, as the first P-51 equipped unit in the 8th AF. Yeager shot down his first Messerschmitt on his seventh mission, one of the early Mustang missions over Berlin, but the next day, 5 March, three Fw 190s shot him down.

## Escape and evasion

Yeager bailed out over occupied France, being careful to delay pulling his ripcord until he had fallen far enough to avoid getting strafed by the German fighters. He landed about fifty miles east of Bordeaux, injured and bleeding, but armed with a pistol. He was determined to make his way over the Pyrenees to Spain. After numerous adventures with the resistance Yeager returned to Britain. Persuading General Eisenhower to allow Yeager to return to combat in the summer of 1944 was difficult, although he managed it.

His mount was now a P-51D nicknamed 'Glamorous Glennis', gaudily decorated in the red and yellow trim of the 357th FG. At first the pickings were slim, as the *Luftwaffe* was licking its wounds after the fierce battles of the summer. He frequently flew in a four-aircraft flight with Bud Anderson and Don Bochkay, two other double aces. On 18 September Yeager flew in support of the *Market Garden* glider drops over Arnhem, but couldn't do much to stop the appalling slaughter of the C-47s. By this time he had been promoted to Lieutenant.

## Ace in a day

Yeager would become an 'ace-in-a-day' on 12 October, while leading a bomber escort over Bremen. As he closed in on one Messerschmitt 109, the pilot broke left and collided with his wingman. Both bailed out, giving Yeager credit for two victories without firing a shot. In the sharp dogfight that followed, Yeager's vision, flying skills, and gunnery ability gave him three more quick kills.

The Messerschmitt 262 jet appeared in combat in the second half of 1944. Its pilots were ordered to attack the bomber streams,

The 'Tuskegee Airmen' of the 332nd FG, 15th AF, made up one of the most unusual of all Mustang outfits. The black pilots of the group had to fight entrenched racial prejudice just to get into combat. However, once in the field with the 15th AF in Italy, they proved as good a fighting group as any. Here, Capt. Andrew D Turner, CO of one of the group's squadrons, listens to Lt Clarence P 'Lucky' Lester describing his third victory. (USAF)

'Glamorous Glen III' is named in honour of the wife of Charles 'Chuck' Yeager, a combat ace over Europe who went on to become a combat commander in post-war Germany and in Vietnam as well as playing a key part in the research flying which contributed to the early years of the space race. Yeager and fellow ace Bud Anderson delighted crowds at a 1995 Warbirds display by making a Mustang fly-past. *(Nicholas A Veronico)*

avoiding dogfights with the escorting fighters wherever possible. Whenever the much more agile Mustangs came close, the jet fighters would open their throttles and pull away from the P-51s using their 100 mph speed advantage. But the jets were vulnerable on landing and take-off, and one day Yeager caught one on final approach. Flying through intense flak he downed the jet and earned a Distinguished Flying Cross for the feat.

He flew his last combat missions in January 1945. He married the Glennis after whom his aircraft were always named in February. He reported to Wright Field in July to start an even more extraordinary career as a test pilot, during which he became the first person to exceed the sound barrier in level flight.

George Preddy was one of the most successful pilots in the 352nd FG when he was

tragically killed in action. General John C Meyer, who was the fourth-ranking American ace in the European war and Preddy's squadron commander for more than a year, wrote: 'George was small and slight. He was soft-spoken, without even a hint of bravado, but I have never met a man of such intense desire to succeed. George Preddy was the complete fighter pilot.'

## Barnstormer-turned-ace

Preddy grew up in Greensboro, North Carolina, where he earned a living before the war as a barnstormer pilot. During 1940 he made three unsuccessful attempts to join the US Navy and was rejected each time because of physical problems. Eventually in December 1942 he managed to join the USAAF. He was assigned to Mitchell Field, NY with No. 1 Fighter

Allison-engined P-51A Mustangs and A-36 Apaches played a vital part in supporting deep-penetration operations in Burma. Special forces like Wingate's Chindits and Merrill's Marauders could only be supplied from the air, and Mustangs escorted transport flights and made pinpoint attacks on Japanese positions in the jungle. Under the command of experienced fighter pilot Colonel Philip Cochran, seen here mounting his P-51A late in 1944, the 1st Air Commando Group was a composite force of fighters, bombers, transports, gliders, light planes and helicopters which provided reconnaissance, combat air patrol, air landing, troop-carrying, interdiction, close air support, resupply, and medevac to the Chindit force. *(USAF)*

Command before moving on to Westover Field, Massachusetts to join a fighter squadron. He met up with IB 'Jack' Donaldson, who he had known in Australia before the war, and calling in some favours, managed to be assigned to the 487th FS, 352nd FG.

Preddy's new Commanding Officer, Colonel John C Meyer, was not impressed by the small size and meekness of Preddy. 'This fellow couldn't punch his way out of a paper bag', is what Meyer said of Preddy after they first met.

In July 1943, the 352nd FG, nicknamed the 'Blue-Nosed Bastards' were based at Bodney. Preddy went on his first combat mission in the ETO in September 1943 and scored his first victory, against a Messerschmitt Bf 109, on 1 December. Three weeks later he shot down a second in combat against a superior force, a feat he would achieve frequently.

## Shuttle missions

The 352nd FG converted to the P-51 in April 1944. Preddy gained his fifth victory on 13 May and was well on his way to becoming the leading active ace in the ETO. By this time the veterans had left the field; Gabreski was a POW and Johnson had gone home. Escorting B-17 bombers to Magdeburg on 20 June, Preddy shot down an Fw 190 and shared an Me 410 with Lieutenant James Woods. On 21 June, the 352nd FG accompanied the 4th FG to Russia for a series of escort operations, the target being the Balkans. On 18 July the 352nd FG would claim twenty-one kills, four of them falling to the guns of George Preddy, whose mind was now well and truly tuned to the tricks of the enemy.

Major Preddy was scheduled to lead the entire group on an escort mission on 6 August. The mission was temporarily suspended due to forecast bad weather. Preddy partied hard that night, so when shortly after midnight the mission was rescheduled for the following day, it came as something of a shock. At crew-briefing, the group commander judged that hung-over Preddy was not in any condition to fly lead, but was persuaded that he would be all right by take-off.

A few hours later at an altitude of 30,000 feet George Preddy spotted more than thirty Messerschmitts attacking a B-17 bomber box formation. He led his flight into the midst of the 109s, shooting down three in rapid succession. At that point four other P-51s engaged the enemy, causing a further distraction which enabled Preddy to shoot down two more enemy fighters. He then followed the formation down to 5,000 feet, where he found himself alone with the enemy. One of them broke to the left, followed by Preddy in his personal Mustang, 'Cripes A'Mighty'. After intense combat George shot down his sixth enemy fighter of the day. On landing, a slightly green Preddy vowed never again to fly with a hangover. For his conduct during this mission he was awarded the Distinguished Service Cross – and an unsought period of leave back home in the United States.

Preddy returned to the ETO in October 1944 as CO of the 328th FS. Whilst leading the squadron on 2 November he and his fellow pilots engaged a formation of Me 109s, downing no fewer than twenty-five.

George Preddy would undertake his final sortie on Christmas Day 1944. As the squadron overflew American ground forces his aircraft was hit by friendly fire which caused his aircraft to crash, Preddy being killed in the impact. By that time, George Preddy had scored over twenty-six confirmed victories, only exceeded by Gabreski and Johnson.

## Tactical Mustangs

The 8th Air Force was not the only American organisation operating out of Britain which produced combat aces flying the Mustang. Although the 9th Air Force mainly concentrated on tactical ground-attack missions, it also produced high-scoring pilots.

One of the most famous was Lieutenant-Colonel James H Howard, commanding the 356th FS, 354th FG based at Boxted, who shot down at least six German aircraft to add to his tally of seven confirmed Japanese victories over Burma and China in 1943. Whilst on an escort mission for a group of B-17s Howard managed single-handedly to break up a concentrated fighter attack on the bombers, for which he was awarded the only Medal of Honour given in the ETO. At least one other pilot would become an ace in the 9th AF. Before being killed in action on 7 July 1944 Lieutenant Donald M Beerbower of the 353rd FS, 354th FG had notched up fifteen and a half victories.

The main user of the Mustang in the Pacific was the USAAF's VII Fighter Command. Flying into Iwo Jima even before the last of the Japanese defenders were defeated, the P-51Ds and P-47Ns of the command were tasked with flying 1,600-mile round-trips in defence of the Boeing B-29 Superfortresses of XXI Bomber Command. With a victory count of 11, Major Robert W Moore was the top-scoring Mustang ace over Japan. *(USAF)*

On the other side of the world the 530th FBS took its P-51A Mustangs into battle against the Japanese in the China-Burma-India Theatre of Operations. Their mission in 1943 included bomber escort as well as ground attack. At this they were eminently successful, so much in fact that the Japanese broadcaster 'Tokyo Rose' named them the 'Yellow Scorpions'. The yellow came from the nose colour which had been applied to stop friendly anti-aircraft gunners

taking pot shots at them. Squadron commander Major James J England had ten confirmed aerial kills and one confirmed ground kill at the end of his tour. In the final tally at war's end he was ranked as the fifth-highest scorer in the 14th Air Force.

Still flying the P-51A in 1944, the squadron continued to rack up considerable success, which in turn created more combat aces. One of these was Lieutenant Lester Arasmith, who

'Stump Jumper' is a genuine veteran of combat operations over Europe, having served with the 357th Fighter Group. After being retired the P-51 was returned to America and placed on display at Norton AFB. Declared surplus in 1965, it was first restored to its wartime glory before being refinished as 'Angels Playmate', once the mount of Bruce Carr, who scored 15 air-to-air victories. (Real Wings Photographs)

scored at least five confirmed victories during his tour. He was also one of the first Mustang pilots to enter the fray in Korea in 1950.

Late in 1944 the unit acquired P-51B/Cs, and continued its combat successes. Aces during this period included Captain Robert Mulhollen and Major L R Reeves, who finished the war with six victories each. The squadron flew 3,671 missions, scoring 109 confirmed victories with a further 53 probables in the air, while 152 enemy aircraft were confirmed destroyed on the ground with a further 61 probables.

With the end of the Second World War and after a brief revival in Korea, the Mustang's front-line career with the US Air Force quickly came to a close. However, the aircraft remained an effective combat machine, and found a ready

market in the air forces of the world. This in turn would create a pool of survivors for the ever growing Warbird community.

To an outsider, these engineers and pilots carry out miracles of restoration to return vintage airframes to the skies. The task requires an immense amount of dedication and skill and no little outlay of cash on the part of the enthusiasts. A whole industry has grown up around this niche market, and if the money is available restoration organisations of whatever size can use refurbished components or they can buy in completely new, often hand-made parts. The depth of skill is such that most airframes are returned to flight in 'as new' condition, with zero hours on the clock.

The United States has a vast number of

P-51Ds 'Ridge Runner III' and 'Ho Hun' perform in formation for the camera, high above California. Although only a small percentage of the thousands of Mustangs built have survived in airworthy condition, it is probably the most numerous of all warbirds. 'Ho Hun' is a P-51D-30NT owned by William Hane of Mesa, Arizona, while 'Ridge Runner III' is a P-51D-20NA operated by Dan Martin of Hollister, California. *(Nicholas A Veronico)*

One of the most modified Mustangs ever constructed is the RB-51, 'Red Baron', designed for high-speed racing. It was powered by a Rolls-Royce Griffon engine, driving a contra-rotating propeller assembly which was counteracted by a fin and rudder of broader chord. This aircraft managed to set a piston-engined world record of 499 mph, although it would be badly damaged in a crash in September 1999. (Real Wings Photographs)

people dedicated to restoring warbirds. One of these organisations is Fighter Enterprises, which is devoted to rebuilding aircraft to order for various clients. One of their best-known rebuilds is P-51D, 'Sizzlin Liz', which underwent a total remanufacture of the airframe, instruments, fuel system, canopy glasses and all systems. The powerplant went to Vintage V-12s based at Tehachapi in California for a complete overhaul. Eventually the reworked components were brought together, reassembled and successfully test-flown. The culmination of all this hard work came when 'Sizzlin Liz' was awarded the Grand Champion Warbird prize for pilot/owner Dave Marco at the 1991 Experimental Aircraft Association meet at Oshkosh, Wisconsin.

In Britain one of the best-known restorers is Rob Lamplough, whose Aerial Museum is renowned for converting absolute wrecks into pristine flying machines. One of these was a P-51D Mustang that was recovered from Israel.

Serialled 44-72216, it was discovered that this particular machine had a history with the 352nd FG of the 8th Air Force, better known as the 'Blue Noses'. This aircraft had been the mount of Captain Ray Littge, whose combat record included thirteen confirmed victories. It was therefore no surprise that the Mustang was refinished in this livery.

Of course, there are other restorers and rebuilders around the world who have either returned the Mustang to stock standard or have created some of the most impressive racing aircraft to grace the pylons and skies of Reno. For the latter the engineers have called in aerodynamic experts to create the ultimate racing machines, with refined airframes, changed or uprated engines and advanced propeller assemblies.

Whatever their purpose, the efforts that restorers expend to recreate the veterans as new stand as a fitting tribute to more than half a century of service from the Mustang.

# 4. Combat Zone: The Fighting Mustang

The biggest user of the North American Mustang in all its forms was the USAAF and its post war successor, the USAF. As already related, the first version to enter service was the A-36A Apache dive bomber, which paved the way for the fighter versions that followed. When the United States Army Air Force first began to arrive in Britain in 1942 to begin operations against Hitler's Germany, they were at a disadvantage. Although the war in and over Europe had been raging for three years, the Americans lacked real combat experience. Civil disorder suppression in the Philippines and some desperate fighting across various Pacific islands in the aftermath of Pearl Harbor was not enough to suit the war that they were about to enter.

## Daylight bombing

The concept behind the tactics to be employed by the 8th AF centred upon its bomber wings carrying out raids against strategic targets across Europe in daylight. The American high command had formulated its strategic approach in the 1930s, when the introduction of the Boeing B-17 had given the Air Corps a bomber which was as fast as contemporary fighters like the Boeing P-26 'Peashooter', and which had excellent high-altitude performance. Coupled with the introduction of the Norden bombsight, which promised great accuracy of ordnance delivery from those heights, the air staff became firm believers in the notion that 'the bomber will always get through'. Escorting fighters would not be necessary, since the heavily armed bombers would fly in tight formations which could bring dozens or even hundreds of heavy machine-guns to bear on enemy fighters.

They ignored the RAF's horrific experience of flying unescorted missions by daylight. The *Luftwaffe*'s fast cannon-armed fighters, flown by some of the best combat pilots in the world, had forced the British out of the daylight skies over Europe. Bomber Command switched to night operations, with streams of Stirlings, Lancasters and Halifaxes delivering huge tonnages of explosive against area targets.

Although Air Vice-Marshal Arthur Harris, Chief of Bomber Command, had warned his counterparts about the extreme danger they would face, the hierarchy of the 8th and 9th Air Forces were initially slow to heed his advice. Early raids against French targets seemed to vindicate the American strategy, but matters changed when strikes were extended deeper into enemy-held territory. Operating without escort in the teeth of the German defences would prove incredibly costly, as the massed bomber formations were hammered and harassed constantly by flak and fighters, both on the way into the target and on the way back. Add the constant fatigue of travelling for hours in a shaking, rattling, noisy bomber coupled with extreme cold at altitude, and the odds were stacked against a bomber crew surviving unscathed through an entire tour.

Obviously such a state of affairs and the heavy losses incurred could not be allowed to continue, since bombers and crews were being lost at an alarming rate. There were genuine fears that even the massive American war machine with its huge new Boeing and Consolidated plants would not be able to keep up the production rate needed to supply replacements. Even more frighteningly, crew losses were not only draining the training schools but were sapping the morale of the crews already in theatre.

As a short-term solution, the bomber groups evolved larger formations to provide even more defensive fire. Initially bombing in flights of three, the B-17s and B-24s were soon flying as squadrons and then as combat boxes – eighteen aircraft from a single bomb group spread across both horizontal and the vertical planes. Ultimately the largest formation used was the combat wing, consisting of two or three combat boxes totalling up to 54 aircraft. Several combat wings would be employed on a major raid.

## Bomber losses

Although bomber crews claimed great success in driving off attacking *Luftwaffe* fighters, the Germans evolved tactics which more than countered the massed American guns. *Luftwaffe* fighters attacked head-on at high speed, with the aim of disrupting the formations and cutting individual bombers out of the boxes. The USAAF sustained increasing losses, culminating in the murderous raids on the Schweinfurt ball-bearing industry.

The solution to the problem was the escort fighter. Unfortunately, the British fighter available in most numbers, the Spitfire, lacked the range to escort bombers further than France or the Dutch coast. The first examples of the North American Mustang were then coming into service, but while they had excellent range, the limitations of their Allison engines meant that above 11,000 feet their performance was limited, and at 30,000 feet they were at a severe disadvantage against the Messerschmitt Bf 109.

The massive Republic P-47 Thunderbolt and Lockheed P-38 Lightning were already in service with the 6th and 3rd Fighter Groups respectively. However, both had limitations. Although the P-47 was a superb fighter, for all its size it lacked the range to escort the bombers all the way to the target. The lack of range was frustrating to the P-47 pilots as they could see the *Luftwaffe* fighters loitering just past their point-of-no-return to attack the bombers. This left the bomber groups on their own to fly and fight their way to the target. While desperate measures were undertaken to improve the Thunderbolt's range, the escort groups did what they could to protect the bombers on the way out and back. The appearance of the Thunderbolts, although welcome, was too little to protect the heavies, so VIII Fighter Command cast around for an aircraft worthy of the bombers.

## Lightning escorts

The appearance of the P-38 Lightning on the inventory of VIII Fighter Command promised much. Here was a fighter which seemed ideal for the mission. The Lightning was fast and had the necessary range, and much was expected of the twin-engined, twin-boomed machine.

Initially the escorts had made a big impact, but soon were suffering at the hands of the *Luftwaffe*. It was the dampness and cold that would defeat the P-38 over Europe as much as the efforts of the German pilots. Unfortunately, the big fighters were powered by Allison engines, effective at low level, but unreliable in the high-altitude fighting over Germany.

During the approach to the target the fighters normally cruised with the bombers, with engines running at average throttle settings. The trouble started when enemy fighters were spotted and the throttles were advanced. Sluggish lubricating oil struggled to do its job properly, turbo-superchargers malfunctioned and the Lightning failed to perform as required. Often the result was the complete failure of an engine, which made the Lightning vulnerable. To compound this problem the fighters were consuming excessive amounts of oil, which also made engine performance deteriorate.

## Lightning failings

Handling of the P-38 also suffered at these high altitudes as the fighter was extremely sluggish in the roll and had other manoeuvring problems. Although more than capable of holding its own at altitudes below 18,000 feet, the average operating height was in the 26,000 to 30,000 feet range with an outside air

Daylight bombing brought the B-17s and B-24s of the 8th Air Force up against the toughest air defences in the world. After negotiating barrages by heavy and light flak artillery, the bombers had to face repeated attacks by highly trained pilots in high-performance fighters, expertly guided by a comprehensive radar network. This bomber has been hit by flak and has drifted under the bombs of another Fortress. *(USAF)*

temperature of −50°C. Lightnings were frequently bounced by Bf 109s diving down from 35,000 feet or higher. To make matters worse, Lightning pilots suffered a cockpit heating system which was basically inadequate for the task. Pilots were so cold that they were often incapable of flying their aircraft to the best of their abilities.

This situation could not be allowed to continue, as losses amongst the bombers and escorting fighters began to mount. It came to a head late in the summer of 1943 when, of a 1,000-bomber fleet, ten per cent were shot down, a loss of over a thousand men. The situation was now serious enough that the possibility of failure was being mooted at high-level meetings towards the end of 1943. Not

only were the 8th Air Force organisations taking excessive losses of men and machines, the morale of those who actually had to do the fighting was beginning to suffer again. In other words something had to be done.

## Mustangs as escorts

That something was to be the introduction of the P-51 Mustang to the Fighter Groups. The irony is that the P-51 was already in use with the USAAF in Britain, having been brought over to equip the fighter squadrons of the tactically oriented 9th Air Force. Eventually a swap was organised between the fighter commands of the two air forces. The Eighth would lose its Thunderbolts to the Ninth in exchange for their Mustangs, whilst the P-38

The only fighters in RAF service which had the range to escort the early missions of the 8th AF bomber force were the P-51As flown by Army Co-operation Command. However, range was not all that was required: USAAF doctrine called for bombing from high altitude, and the Allison-powered P-51As would have been at a serious disadvantage against the *Luftwaffe's* Bf 109s. The bombers had to wait until the Merlin-Mustangs arrived before they could be reliably escorted all the way to the target. *(C P Russell Smith Collection)*

Lightnings would be transferred to the Pacific, a theatre much more suited to their qualities.

The Mustang had arrived in Britain in late 1943. The P-51Bs had a range capability far greater than was necessary in the tactical missions for which they were first used.

## Tactical missions

During their time with the 9th Air Force the Mustangs had been engaged in escorting the aircraft of the Tactical Bomber Groups to targets mainly concentrated in France, although side trips to the Netherlands were sometimes added to spice up the menu. Their principal charges were B-26 Marauders, fast medium bombers operating at much lower altitudes than the B-17s of the 8th Air Force. After the big change-over the Ninth used the mighty P-47 in a similar manner, achieving outstanding results with the beefy Republic machine as a fighter-bomber alongside the RAF's Typhoons.

Whilst the groups of the Ninth were enjoying the benefits of the P-51 their opposite numbers in the Eighth were struggling to cope with the demands of long-range bomber escort using the equipment to hand. For the 8th Air Force and the hard-pressed VIII Fighter Command, the P-51 Mustang was a revelation. Here was a fighter that had the range, speed and manoeuvrability to take on any opponent. From this point bomber escort operations would be transformed and the bond between the Flying Fortresses and Liberators and their 'Little Friends' would become stronger still.

The man responsible for changing the fighter fortunes of the 8th Air Force was Lieutenant-Colonel Donald Blakeslee. As the Deputy Commanding Officer of the 4th Fighter Group he managed to wangle a series of semi-official visits to Boxted airfield near Colchester to fly the newly arrived P-51B Mustang. Don Blakeslee was an experienced combat fighter pilot with a prodigious number of flying hours and over 120 combat sorties as a volunteer with the RAF, which were then followed by further missions when the Eagle squadrons became part of the USAAF. The test flights, which were in truth combat missions, would enthuse Don Blakeslee greatly. In his report to higher command he recommended that the P-51 be assigned to the 4th FG and those other units that were due to form.

## Merlin advantages

The positives in his report centred upon the engine installation, fuel contents and agility of the aircraft. In contrast to both the Allison-powered Mustangs and the P-38 Lightning the Rolls-Royce engine installed in the P-51B was more than capable of operating at the heights called for by bomber escort work. Not only could a top cover above the bomber boxes be

maintained, the powerplant was much more reliable than the Allison engines, though early missions encountered the usual teething troubles. Another much needed bonus which came with the Merlin-Mustang was an excellent all-round performance, a high top speed at all altitudes and an outstanding rate of climb.

For such a small aircraft the Mustang could pack in an incredible amount of fuel. The economy of the Packard-built Merlin 61 engine meant that the 184 gallons packed into the fighter's wing tanks could carry the airframe some 300 miles. When the rear fuselage tank containing 85 gallons was added this raised the range to 475 miles, which was 100 miles more than the P-47 Thunderbolt. A further increase in

Each of the USAAF's three great fighters, seen here in formation at the end of the war, had its strengths and weaknesses. The Republic P-47 Thunderbolt was a big, beefy machine, which could fly escort missions but which was also a superb fighter-bomber. The speedy twin-boomed Lockheed P-38 Lightning had a long range, and its twin engines added a safety factor to the long over-water missions in the Pacific. The Mustang was a superb all-rounder, with speed, range and agility, only lacking the P-47's toughness in ground-attack missions. *(USAF)*

range would be gained when auxiliary tanks were installed. Rated at 75 gallons each, these would give the Mustang the unheard of range of 650 miles, which was incredible for a single-engined fighter in Europe. Originally the wing pylons were only capable of carrying bombs, but a modification programme by the Air Technical Section soon added plumbing for fuel transfer. As with the earlier tanks fitted to the P-47, the Mustang system required an air pressure feed to force the fuel out of the tanks.

## Gentle persuasion

Don Blakeslee's enthusiastic report did not mean that the 9th Air Force's Mustangs were instantly transferred to the fighter groups of their long-range rival. As an interim measure, gentle pressure was applied to the Ninth to provide some escort missions for the bombers of the Eighth. Eventually, all new P-51s would be assigned to No. VIII Fighter Command, 8th Air Force, whilst the Ninth would receive the P-47 Thunderbolts.

Although the primary role of the Mustangs within the 8th Air Force was one of bomber escort, they also found time to carry out ground-strafing attacks, particularly after the bombers had started for home. This was dangerous, since in addition to the often lethal German light flak, pilots might encounter the barely understood phenomenon of target fixation – the pilot would be concentrating so intensely on his attack that he would forget to pull up out of a dive. In fact at least one Mustang made it back to base after a ground-attack raid where the propeller had touched the ground, causing the tips to bend over. However, such was the strength of the airframe and the reliability of the engine that the P-51B managed to reach Manston safely. Additionally, the P-51's radiator system, exposed on the underside of the aircraft, was vulnerable to ground fire.

The period surrounding the D-Day landings would see the Mustangs engaged in Operation *Neptune*, supporting the invasion of Europe.

This portrait of a P-51D Mustang on a pre-delivery test flight reveals some interesting details. Under the rear fuselage it would appear that an anti-static discharge wick has been fitted whilst the small, flush air intake under the exhausts has a mesh filter installed as standard. Early Mustangs in Europe suffered some teething troubles, notably with unreliable spark plugs. British plugs seemed to last longer, and once the USAAF established an adequate supply the problem virtually disappeared. *(C P Russell Smith Collection)*

One shot from what is possibly the most famous of all Mustang photo sequences shows a flight from the 375th FS, 361st FG over Europe in July 1944. Farthest from the camera is a P-51B, accompanied by three P-51Ds. The two central aircraft are early 'Ds', since they lack the dorsal fillet seen on the nearest machine. *(USAF)*

Carrying the black and white recognition stripes worn by all Allied aircraft, the P-51s operating from Britain all had distinct roles during the invasion. Ninth Air Force fighters were assigned to fly high cover above the Beachhead, whilst those of the Eighth would act in support of the troops moving off the landing zones and to stave off the attentions of any enemy fighters at an altitude of 8,000 feet. Their RAF counterparts would be operating beneath, in direct support of the troops.

## Normandy ground attack

There was little air-to-air action for the Mustang pilots, since any reinforcements the *Luftwaffe* could send to the front were often destroyed on their airfields by overwhelmingly superior Allied air power. As a result, the P-51s spent much of their time in ground-strafing, dive-bombing and providing regular battlefield patrols.

As the landings were proceeding according to plan from an air force point of view, it was realised that putting further pressure upon German forces on a different front might cause further disruption and bring the war to a speedier conclusion. To this end a force of B-17 Flying Fortresses accompanied by Mustang fighters was despatched to Russia. Except for a small entanglement with some marauding Fw 190s the whole force landed almost intact. One Mustang had been shot down, while another had diverted to Kiev after becoming lost. To support the P-51s a skeleton group of maintenance crews had flown in the B-17s where they acted as waist gunners. Tools and necessary spares had been carried in the rear fuselages of the bombers. After arrival the bombers and fighters were prepared for their mission, which was aimed at the German units in the Balkans. The whole mission proceeded almost without incident and the fighters finally landed in Italy after many hours airborne.

While the Allies advanced through Normandy, the daylight bombing of Germany continued. It was during this period that the attacking aircraft met the new menace of jet- and rocket-powered fighters. The first sightings were of the rocket-powered Messerschmitt Me 163 Komet, the first of which was encountered near Merseburg on 29 July 1944. The first Mustang losses to the Messerschmitts of 1./JG 400 occurred a few days later, when three P-51s of the 352nd FG were shot down. This obviously raised some concern amongst the Mustang pilots. Accustomed as they had become to mastery of the skies, an enemy with so much speed advantage was a real worry. The answer appeared to be extra vigilance and detailing specific fighters to attack the rocket fighters as they appeared. During the first such action, the defending fighters managed to ambush two of the Me 163s and shoot them down, whilst another two were reported as damaged.

## The Jet threat

The other Messerschmitt fighter that appeared at about the same time was far more effective. This was the jet-powered Me 262, which had originally been misused by Hitler, who had personally ordered that the superb new fighter be used as a bomber. At a stroke, the astonishing machine made the Mustang and all other piston-engined fighters obsolete. However, it was not invincible. Its engines had a designed service life of around twenty hours, and they often failed after six or seven hours. The engines were also unforgiving of hard throttle use, so the 262s were vulnerable if they could be jumped soon after take-off or landing, while they were travelling at slow speeds.

In order to combat this new menace all efforts were concentrated upon discovering their home airfields, the plan being to attack the

Me 262s on the ground. Overall this strategy was successful, as many were caught on the ground whilst others were intercepted during take-off and landing. Lieutenant Urban L Drew shot down two jets in a single engagement in October 1944. Several other pilots brought down jets, including Captain Charles 'Chuck' Yeager, who in 1947 would become famous as the man who broke the sound barrier.

## Recon Mustangs

Whilst the fighter pilots were fending off the *Luftwaffe*, another group were flying the F-6 reconnaissance version of the Mustang on missions that were just as hazardous. Not only did these pilots have to contend with enemy fighters and flak, there was also the added hazard of target fixation as the occasional loss would proclaim. Their primary role was that of tactical reconnaissance over the battlefield, and although the 9th Air Force was the main user, the Eighth also used a few recce birds. Two versions of the F-6 were operated. The first was a production version built at Inglewood, whilst the second was a field modification. Both featured oblique and vertical cameras for greater terrain coverage.

When German forces finally surrendered in 1945, the only thought the Mustang crews had was to return home to the United States. No. VIII Fighter Command of the 8th Air Force finally departed from Britain in March 1946 when the airfield at Honington was returned to Royal Air Force control. During its service with the USAAF the P-51 Mustang became known as the fighter that changed the war in Europe. Given its range, speed and airborne agility this seems a fitting epithet for such a significant aircraft.

## Mediterranean action

While the P-51 was creating an everlasting reputation for itself over Europe, the versatile North American design was also playing a major part in the battles in other theatres. The first version into service with the USAAF was the A-36A, which primarily served with North-west African Air Forces and American forces in the Far East. Originally built with wing-mounted dive brakes for service as a dive bomber, the Apache was almost too fast for the job, and pilots sometimes experienced

Seen from one of the observation blisters of a Boeing B-29 Superfortress, a pair of P-51s of the 15th FG formate on the big bomber on their way to the Japanese home islands. The Mustangs were packed with fuel for the 1,500-mile round-trip, flying at 210 mph for maximum efficiency. Eight hours in a World War Two single-seater was no picnic, and pilots often held long radio conversations with the bombers to help time pass. *(USAF)*

problems in bombing accurately. In level flight or a shallow dive the A-36 was far more successful and accurate. Coupled to the available bomb load was the wing-mounted armament which presented a complete ground-attack package to the USAAF commanders.

The first pure fighter version was the P-51A Mustang, which was primarily employed in the Far East region on escort duties by the 311th Fighter-Bomber Group. Also operating in the same region was Chennault's 23rd Fighter Group, whose missions included supplying an escort service for groups of B-25 Mitchells on bombing raids against Japanese airfields.

When the Merlin-powered Mustang became available for service issue, units operating in the Mediterranean region under the control of the 15th Air Force also received some to replace earlier equipment. The most famous of these was the 332nd Fighter Group, better known as the all-Negro 'Tuskegee Airmen'. These outstanding fighters accumulated an excellent record whilst undertaking escort duties and ground attack missions as the Allied armies pushed their way laboriously up the mountainous Italian peninsula.

As German forces were being pushed back out of Italy the fighter groups of the 15th AF were re-equipping with the more advanced P-51D version of the Mustang. These were plumbed for the long-range escort mission from the outset by the area Air Technical Branch. This allowed 15th Air Force Mustangs to fly the longest escort missions of the European war on 25 March 1945, a round-trip from northern Italy to Berlin and back in support of the four-engined heavies of the 15th Air Force. It was during this mission that Colonel William Daniel, CO of the 308th FS, 31st FG, shot down a Messerschmitt Me 262 whilst other aircraft from the same group also managed to shoot down or damage six others.

## Far East Mustangs

The long-range missions in Europe were matched by those flown by Mustangs in the Pacific. The first P-51s were assigned to the 5th Air Force in the south-west Pacific early in 1945, where they made their combat debut in the Philippines. In March, the first P-51s of the 7th Air Force landed on Iwo Jima while the last of the Japanese defenders were still holding

out, and were immediately thrown into the fight against Japanese trenches and pillboxes. However, their primary purpose, and the main reason that Iwo Jima was seized in the first place, was to escort B-29 Superfortresses bombing the Japanese home islands from bases in the Marianas. Mustangs also provided close support for the invasion of Okinawa, and in the last months of the war ranged the skies above Japan, strafing anything that moved.

Whilst the USAAF was operating various versions of the Mustang the RAF was also flying Mustangs Mk I and Mk IA, some of which had been field-modified to act as reconnaissance aircraft. Although the RAF aircraft were allocated to the Army Co-operation role their primary use was that of low-level hit-and-run raids across Europe known as 'Rhubarbs'. These sorties entailed pairs of aircraft flying at high speed and low level to hit targets such as airfields, trains and other targets of interest. The reconnaissance versions also operated in pairs although only one aircraft was primed for photography, the

The need that the USAAF expressed for a long-range fighter would be met by North American, which produced the F-82 to fill the gap. Based on the Mustang airframe, the twin-engined fighter carried a pilot in each cockpit, which helped to share the load on long missions. Later, the type's primary role would change to that of night fighter, which did not call for such long flights, and the right-hand cockpit would lose its duplicate controls in favour of radar displays and navigation equipment. *(C P Russell Smith Collection)*

other being employed as defensive top cover. In this instance the Allison-powered aircraft were operating in their best environment, that of low level in warmer temperatures. When the RAF received the Merlin-powered version of the Mustang this was designated the Mk III and would feature the bulged Malcolm hood which improved all-round vision. The RAF also gained quantities of the bubble-hooded versions equivalent to the P-51D/K which were designated the Mustangs Mk IV and Mk V. All these latter versions were used in the more conventional fighter role.

## Mustangs in Korea

Even with the end of World War Two, the Mustang's combat usage continued. The outbreak of fighting in Korea in 1950, caused by the invasion of the South by the Communist North, meant that the P-51, by now in the veteran class, had to return to fighting a new enemy. The first variant into action was the unusual F-82 Twin Mustang which had originally been conceived as a night/long-range fighter. Although reconfigured for the ground attack role the aircraft was not really suitable for the task and quickly moved back into the roles for which it was designed. In a search for more appropriate aircraft, the United States Air Force, as the USAAF had become in 1947, trawled Air National Guard units to gather together enough F-51 Mustangs to equip a combat wing. Once deployed to Korea the fighters were employed in the ground attack role, for which purpose they were fitted with underwing rocket mounts. The fighter was the primary type deployed to Korea, but since the USAF also needed a tactical reconnaissance presence the RF-51 version was also sent to the Far East. Further support for the Mustangs of the USAF came from the South African Air Force, which deployed No. 2 Sqn SAAF to Korea from September to November 1950.

The SAAF unit, known as the 'Flying Cheetahs', already had great experience in operating Mustangs as the squadron had flown them from Italy during World War Two, achieving more than 100 combat kills in the

Even when on the ground the Mustang had its uses, as this portrait of P-51H 44-64180 shows. After the massive demobilisation of 1945 and 1946, the US armed forces, who had now taken on the role of a global police force, found themselves stretched to meet their worldwide responsibiities. The recruitment message under the cockpit of this Mustang is a straightforward appeal for those with the right skills to join the Air Force to protect the victory so hard won in Europe and the Far East. (C P Russell Smith Collection)

The Air National Guard has long been a replacement pool for the regular US military, and after the war many veteran Mustang pilots kept their skills current as 'Weekend Warriors' flying for the various state organisations. This P-51D of the California ANG is on an air-to-ground training mission. Within a very short time both the aircraft and the pilot skills would be urgently required in Asia, with ANG F-51s forming a key part of the USAF's immediate response to the Northern invasion of South Korea. (C P Russell Smith Collection)

process. Now deployed to Korea, No. 2 Sqn joined up with the American F-51s at K-14, Pyongyang East airfield. In common with the rest of the 18th FG, their duties called for them to range all over Korea in support of ground forces. Primarily armed with bombs and rockets, they also deployed napalm against more stubborn targets.

## Ground attack

No. 2 Sqn and its pilots had a reputation for fighting like terriers and being fearless in the attack, as one event revealed. Having undertaken a wide-ranging patrol that had been very quiet, one of the pilots spotted a North Korean T-34 tank being loaded onto a transporter. One after another the Mustangs peeled off and attacked the vehicles with gunfire and their remaining rockets. By the time the last one pulled clear all the vehicles were smouldering wrecks.

The conduct of the war changed considerably with the appearance of the MiG-15 jet fighter. Once the initial shock of meeting enemy jet aircraft had worn off, the F-51 pilots adopted new tactics to combat the latest menace. The primary method of avoiding trouble was to spot the MiGs at an early stage and head for the ground. This, however, exposed the vulnerable coolant systems to ground fire, as did the task of strafing enemy troops. Losses to the Mustang fleet were high, and eventually all survivors were concentrated within the 18th Fighter Group, all other operators having converted to jets.

Mission priorities had by then changed considerably. Remaining Mustangs were tasked with attacking truck convoys, troop concentrations and ammunition dumps. The purpose behind these sorties was to stop the Chinese forces from building up a stockpile big enough to mount a major offensive.

The days of the Mustang in use with both the USAF and SAAF units became numbered as losses increased. It was decided that these veterans be replaced by the far more advanced

WR-P was a P-51B Mustang on the inventory of the 354th Fighter Squadron, 355th Fighter Group. The bulged-Malcolm hood was a major advance on the original flat-panel canopy, though it was not as effective as the later bubble canopy fitted to the P-51D. The 355th had originally been equipped with P-47s, switching to Mustangs in March 1944. The group claimed 15 out of 26 German aircraft destroyed by the USAAF on D-Day, and it went on to be the 8th AF's most successful ground-strafing unit. *(NAA Archive)*

North American F-86 Sabre. On 31 December 1952 the Mustangs of No. 2 Sqn made a final flypast over the base at Chinhae before they were handed over to a Maintenance Supply Group for disposal.

## Israeli defenders

Other nations also used the Mustang to good effect, some in a most unusual manner. One of these was Israel, whose Israeli Air Force/Defence Force (IAF/DF), by a variety of open and clandestine means, managed to collect Mustangs from all over the globe. The primary unit to fly the P-51 was No. 101 Sqn, whose duties included air patrols and ground attack. Although they were few in number, the P-51s performed reasonably well during the War of Independence in the late 1940s, shooting down at least one opposition aircraft before hostilities ended. Further deliveries of Mustangs allowed the IAF/DF to give a good account of itself during the Suez Crisis, which began on 29 October 1956. Possibly one of their most

unusual missions required a pair of fighters to fly at low level towing drag hooks with which they were to destroy the telephone lines leading from the Egyptian capital, Cairo. This madcap idea was unsuccessful, so the pilots came up with an even stranger scheme. They flew in at low level and cut the wires with their wings! Apart from a few dents the Mustangs returned home without further incident. Soon afterwards the Mustang was retired from Israeli service in favour of French-supplied jets.

Many other nations flew surplus or retired Mustangs, but the P-51's days of escorting bombers through swarms of fighters and walls of flak were long over. From Scandinavia to Latin America, the Mustangs found themselves undertaking similar duties. These normally encompassed Combat Air Patrols and practising bomb and rocket attacks. In Latin America some of these skills were put into use during skirmishes between the various countries and during internal policing and counter-insurgency duties. One of the strangest

On the ground receiving attention to its Packard-built Merlin engine is this P-51D assigned to the 364th Fighter Group. To ensure optimum performance it was standard practice all through the war to change or clean the plugs on the Merlin on a regular basis, since they fouled quite easily. The 364th trained on and flew its first missions in Lockheed P-38 Lightnings, switching to Mustangs in July 1944. *(NAA Archive)*

Lieutenant Darwin L Berry of the 335th FS, 4th FG, sets off from Debden on a mission to eastern Germany – note the long-range drop tanks carried by his Mustang. The 4th FG, formed from the volunteer Eagle Squadrons serving with the RAF in 1941 and 1942, destroyed more enemy aircraft than any other USAAF group. *(USAF)*

Israel bought at least 25 Mustangs in the early 1950s, most coming from Sweden. They were used intensively on ground-attack missions during the 1956 Sinai war, making the very first attacks and seeing almost constant action. Nine aircraft were lost in action, mostly to ground fire. *(Aerospace Archive)*

Resplendent in the gloss black finish of the night fighter, this F-82F of the 52nd FS, 46-433, sports red buzz numbers and pale blue flashes adorned with stars to enliven its otherwise sombre finish. Around 91 examples of the 'F' model were completed, along with 59 of the similar 'G' model which had a different radar fit. The 150 aircraft equipped three all-weather fighter groups and one reserve fighter group. *(USAF)*

of all operational Mustang deployments was in the Haiti of Papa Doc Duvalier – the despotic dictator insisted that the aircraft of his air force flew all of their sorties unarmed, as his greatest fear was their use in a *coup* attempt.

Today many Mustangs are still flying, though without weapons. The last operational F-51s were retired in 1984. The mission of the survivors of today is to race and entertain – a far cry from the classic fighter's desperate heyday in the skies over Nazi Germany, but nevertheless thrilling to the legions of P-51 *aficionados* all over the world.

Possibly the best angle to understand the care that the designers at North American took to streamline their fighter. By the time this RAAF marked example took to the skies even the bomb carriers had undergone a transformation. Australia was a major post-war user of the Mustang, taking delivery of more than 200 ex-USAAF machines, assembling 100 from American parts and building a further 120 under licence. *(Nick Challoner)*

# 5. Mustangs for all Seasons: Versions and Variants

Technically, the Mustang was a clever combination of innovation, experience and the courage to try new ideas. The first impression of the NA-73, on paper at least, showed a low-wing monoplane with a span of just over 35 feet and a fuselage length of just over 32 feet. The prominent features incorporated at this stage included a curved windscreen and early versions of the cowling intake and the original, shallower under-fuselage radiator fairing. A model of this version underwent extensive testing in the California Institute of Technology. This revealed that some changes would be needed to improve the function of the air scoops. The resultant prototype, designated the NA-73X, was rolled out complete with redesigned intakes, but still retained the curved windscreen.

## Aerodynamic refinement

The flight-testing of this aircraft revealed that the laminar-flow wing behaved as required – and that the reworked intakes performed even better than expected. In fact the new fairing gave the prototype Mustang a positive boost, as the gases exhausted from the vent acted as a jet, increasing its top speed. Known as the Meredith effect, it was estimated that this feature gave the Mustang the equivalent of an extra 200 horsepower.

Structurally the prototype and its production siblings were very similar in construction. To streamline the build process the aircraft was manufactured in component parts that would join up as the assembly moved down the production line. Among the major components were the wing sections, which were bolted together to form a single assembly. Separate items that would be added later included the wingtips, ailerons and flaps. Although the wing was laminar in section the construction was fairly conventional. Each wing section had a main spar upon which the undercarriage was hung. Aft of the primary spar was the secondary spar, which not only added strength but helped the wing maintain its shape. On the front face of the main spar were the wing nose ribs that shaped the leading edge, whilst between the two spars were further ribs and stringers that performed a similar function. The tailplane was of similar construction although it was a one-piece unit, as was the fin. The flight surfaces, ailerons, elevator and rudder, were of metal construction and were assembled around a spar and shaping ribs. All were operated by cables, rods and pulleys which came complete with cable guides and tensioners.

The semi-monocoque fuselage consisted of one major and one minor assembly. The former encompassed the greater part of the fuselage, which in turn housed the cockpit and the fuselage fuel tank. Construction featured two solid bulkheads. The forward bulkhead, which also served as the engine mounting, was fireproofed. The rear bulkhead was armoured to protect the pilot. Both had lightening holes which allowed the passage of engine and flying controls. The remainder of the fuselage consisted of frames which were held together using stringers and longerons for structural

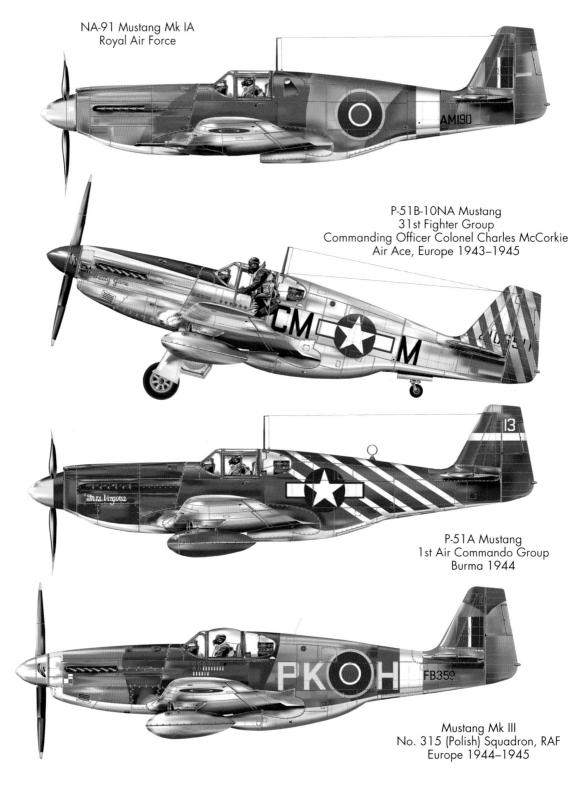

NA-91 Mustang Mk IA
Royal Air Force

P-51B-10NA Mustang
31st Fighter Group
Commanding Officer Colonel Charles McCorkie
Air Ace, Europe 1943–1945

P-51A Mustang
1st Air Commando Group
Burma 1944

Mustang Mk III
No. 315 (Polish) Squadron, RAF
Europe 1944–1945

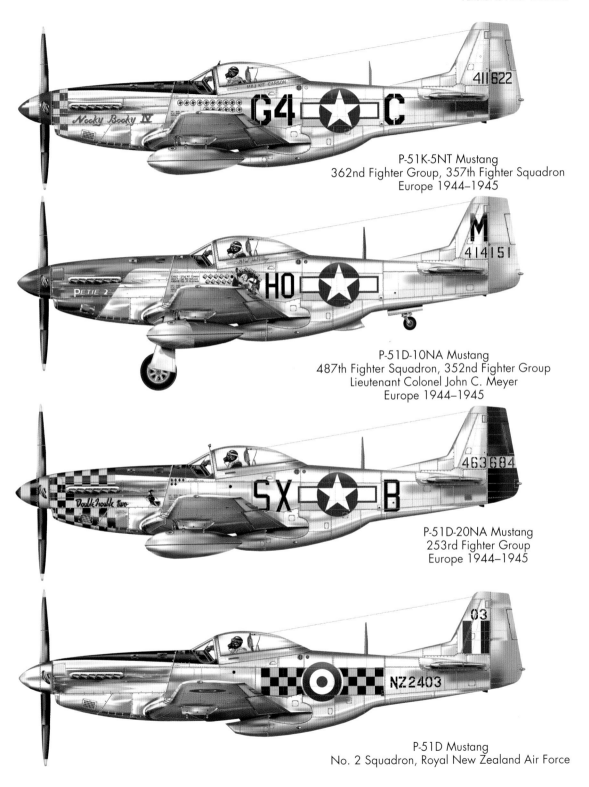

P-51K-5NT Mustang
362nd Fighter Group, 357th Fighter Squadron
Europe 1944–1945

P-51D-10NA Mustang
487th Fighter Squadron, 352nd Fighter Group
Lieutenant Colonel John C. Meyer
Europe 1944–1945

P-51D-20NA Mustang
253rd Fighter Group
Europe 1944–1945

P-51D Mustang
No. 2 Squadron, Royal New Zealand Air Force

strength. The smaller rear fuselage section was used to mount the tailplane, fin, rudder and the tailwheel. It was bolted to the forward fuselage section to form the whole. Over the bones of the Mustang was an aluminium alloy skin.

The engine mountings were completely new, as they deviated from the accepted standard of the day. On most aircraft they consisted of tubular strut support assemblies which cradled the engine on each side. For the Mustang, Art Chester, one of the design team, created a built-up aluminium assembly to hold the Allison powerplant. It later proved equally able to hold the Merlin engine.

## Cooling solutions

Both the Allison and Rolls-Royce products were designed with tight cowlings to provide the smallest frontal area possible, and this in turn led to some interesting solutions for cooling the powerplant. Powerful aero-engines generate a lot of heat, and can be cooled in two ways. The bulky radials preferred by the US military at the time used air cooling, sometimes supplemented by a liquid cooling ring. Inline engines lacked the frontal area to allow the passage of massive quantities of air necessary for cooling, so instead they used liquid cooling, generally utilising glycol-based systems. That of the NA-73X and the Mustang required a large radiator matrix to be positioned under the rear fuselage and housed in an aerodynamic fairing into which the coolant was fed. The initial design created problems with the airflow around the fairing and under the wing. The solution was to stand the intake one inch further out from the airframe, which cured the airflow disturbance.

Unlike the later Merlin engine, the earlier Allison engine required that an extra intake be mounted above the forward cowling to provide air for the carburettor. To be efficient this needed a constant steady airflow. In early models its position and shape caused overheating due to the boundary layer breaking away. A minor change in location and a small extension to the inlet cured the fault.

The first Mustang variant was fitted with a three-bladed propeller and was powered by an Allison V-1710-F3R rated at 1,000 hp at 12,000 feet. The cockpit, although well laid out, was no place for the larger pilot since the Curtiss P-40-

style flat canopy assembly was very close. There were two access hatches built into the canopy assembly, one on the port side and one at the top. In production aircraft the original curved windscreen was replaced by a flat panel screen, later armoured, with curved side panels. The curved screen had caused some visual distortion.

Mounted to the rear of the canopy assembly was the aerial mast. Unfortunately as soon as the first Mustangs passed the 300 mph mark the aerial was torn off. This was because the device had originally been designed for the same company's O-47 spotter aircraft, which travelled at a far slower speed. The cure was discovered very much by accident. An engineer on the development team discovered that, by hammering a piece of steel tube into a tapered aerofoil shape and using it as the aerial, it would stay attached to the airframe with only a minimal increase in drag and loss of speed.

The first production version of the Mustang for the USAAF was an attack version designated the A-36A, which was originally named the Apache. An attempt was made to rename it the Invader, although by war's end it was referred to by one and all as a Mustang. The main change from the prototype was the inclusion of dive brakes on the wings. The nose guns firing through the propeller arc, first tested on the XP-51, remained on the production version although in the field many were removed. Pylons were incorporated under the wings for the carriage of bombs.

## Mustang fighters

After the fighter-bomber came the first pure fighter, the RAF's Mustang Mk I and the USAAF's P-51. Allison-powered fighters were similar to the A-36A, retaining the nose guns, but the airbrakes were dispensed with. The primary difference between the pair was that the RAF version carried an oblique camera mounted behind the port rear view canopy panel with another mounted vertically in the lower fuselage.

Following on from the Mk I was the very similar Mk IA, whose main feature was the deletion of the machine guns in the nose and wings in favour of four 20-mm cannon in the wings. A further change of fixed armament to

Unusually this P-51A Mustang wears RAF camouflage and USAAC-style national markings, which were discarded in the spring of 1942. It is likely that this airframe was one of the two Mustang Is from the original British order which were held back by the US military. Under the designation XP-51B, these aircraft were tested at Wright Field in the last half of 1941, but little real interest was shown. *(C P Russell Smith Collection)*

four machine-guns in the wings and an uprated Allison engine resulted in the appearance of the Mustang Mk II and the P-51A.

## Rolls-Royce Power

Once the Rolls-Royce Merlin engine was fitted to the P-51 airframe, the Mustang became a changed and more versatile aircraft. To absorb the extra power a four-bladed propeller assembly was fitted instead of the original three-bladed unit. The installed powerplant was manufactured by Packard and had a rating of 1,520 hp. The extra power came in part from a two-stage, two-speed supercharger with aftercooler. The original engine mount could handle the extra power, but some structural strengthening was required throughout the rest of the airframe.

As the fighter's rate of roll had increased, improved and reinforced ailerons were installed. The external weapons pylons were also redesigned, being given a more streamlined shape and an increased carrying capability. The early Merlin versions produced for the USAAF were designated the P-51B and C, depending on whether they were built at Inglewood or Dallas, whilst that for the RAF became known as the Mustang Mk III. Later in the career of the RAF versions the Malcolm sliding hood replaced the earlier flat-sided installation. This was a significant change as it improved pilot visibility and escape possibilities, and was adopted by a number of USAAF units in Europe.

To replace the high-backed Mustangs, North American developed the P-51D. The most obvious physical change was the reduction of the rear fuselage and the replacement of the

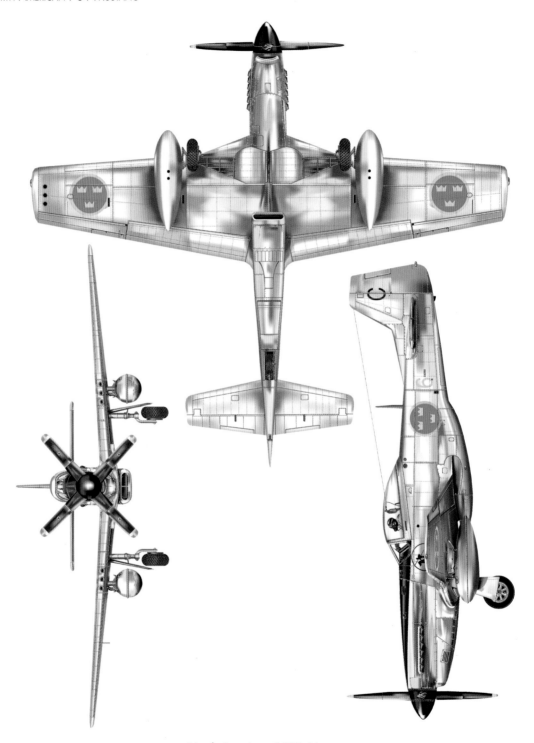

North American P-51D Mustang
F16 Swedish Air Force

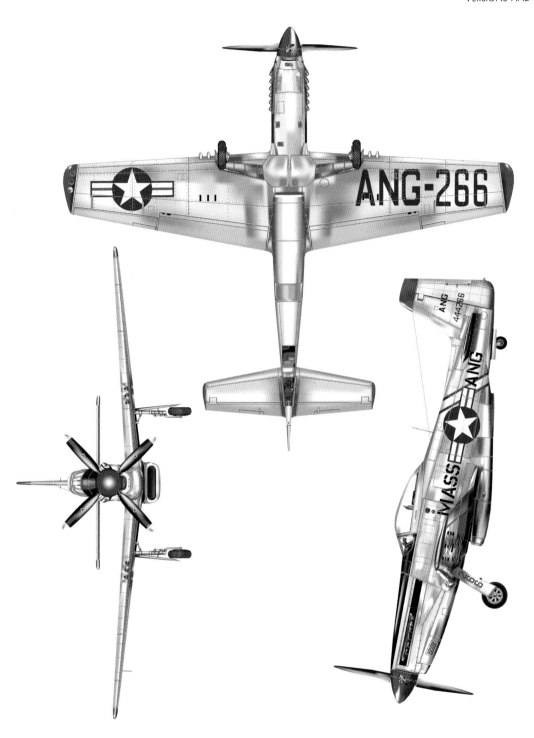

North American F-51H Mustang
Massachusetts Air National Guard

earlier canopy with a bubble, or blister, canopy. The fixed armament was set at six machine-guns, all housed in the wings whilst the pylons under the wings were plumbed to take both bombs and fuel tanks. Changing the contours of the fuselage caused a slight longitudinal stability problem that was fixed by the addition of a small dorsal fin fillet. This particular version was known as the Mustang IV in Royal Air Force service. In a similar manner to the P-51B/C models the bubble-hooded Mustangs built at the NAA Dallas plant were designated as the P-51K. The only difference between the types was that the Texas-built airframes sported an Aero Products propeller instead of the Hamilton Standard Hydromatic unit installed on the P-51D built in California.

## Lightweight Mustangs

Prior to the appearance of the lighter P-51H North American had run through a series of experimental versions of the Mustang. Most were a product of the attempt to create an extremely lightweight fighter known as the XP-51F. This was a total redesign of the Mustang, and none of the structural components were compatible with earlier versions of the P-51. At the core of the redesign was a new low-drag wing complete with a refined planform. The fuselage also underwent some streamlining with an improved fuselage, revised radiator fairing contours and lightened engine mountings. The undercarriage was redesigned as was the hydraulic system. Engine cooling was revamped with the radiator being replaced by an oil cooler unit. Pilot ergonomics also came into consideration with the cockpit heating being reworked and the panel was redesigned for better ease of use. To further lighten the overall weight the gun armament was reduced to four machine-guns whilst the fuel load was also reduced. This particular airframe was never developed beyond the prototype stage, although some of features developed for it would appear in the follow-on XP-51G and in later production models.

'Lou IV' was an early P-51D flown by Colonel Thomas J J Christian Jr, commanding officer of the 361st Fighter Group. Operating from Bottisham, the group had switched from P-47s to P-51Bs in May 1944, and by the time of the Normandy invasion was starting to receive 'D' models. Until July 1944, group aircraft had a thin yellow band around the front of the cowling; Christian's aircraft was one of the first in which the yellow was extended back to the cockpit. On 12 August 1944, within days of this photo being taken, the aircraft would be destroyed and Christian killed after being shot down while strafing. (USAF)

The P-51H version of the Mustang was a successful attempt to improve the type by incorporating features developed in a number of experimental lightweight airframes. Not only did the aircraft lose weight, but the wing, fin, rudder and engine cooling system were redesigned. These changes gave the Mustang an even more sprightly performance, taking maximum speed up to more than 480 mph at 25,000 feet. *(C P Russell Smith Collection)*

Whilst the majority of Mustangs flew with the Merlin engine, there were those within North American who felt that the Allison Engine Company's products should be given a second look. The result was the construction of a pair of Mustangs known as the XP-51J, both of which were powered by the Allison V-1710-119. This engine gave a basic output of 1,500 hp, similar to the contemporary Merlin, although this could be increased to 1,720 hp with water injection. A dorsal fin was fitted for stability, whilst the inlet for the injection-type carburettor was redesigned to reduce its drag. All three experimental versions of the Mustang were considered unsuitable for front-line service as they would require more resources to maintain than the in-service P-51D. The work put into these aircraft eventually resulted in the P-51H.

North American developed the P-51H to follow on from the P-51D. This had been evolved from the XP-51G prototype, and required the extension of the fuselage by 12 inches to counteract the heavier weight of the uprated Packard V-1650-9 engine. This powerplant was capable of a maximum output of 2,000 hp due to the availability of water injection and a change to 150-octane fuel. The tail surfaces were completely redesigned, and further changes resulted in a lighter airframe. As before, the armament was six machine-guns carried in the wings whilst the external weapons-load capability was increased to carry ten 0.5-inch rockets or two bombs or fuel tanks.

## Final Mustangs

Two other variants of the Mustang were to be produced. The first was the P-51L, which was an upgraded P-51H that featured a Packard V-1650-11 powerplant. An initial order for the Model NA-129, consisting of 1,700 airframes, was placed just before the end of the war, but cessation of hostilities saw its swift cancellation. Another version that suffered the same fate was the P-51M, which was to be built at the Dallas plant of NAA. The powerplant was intended to be the Packard V-1650-9A. In contrast to the P-51L, at least one airframe was completed, although the other 1,628 were cancelled.

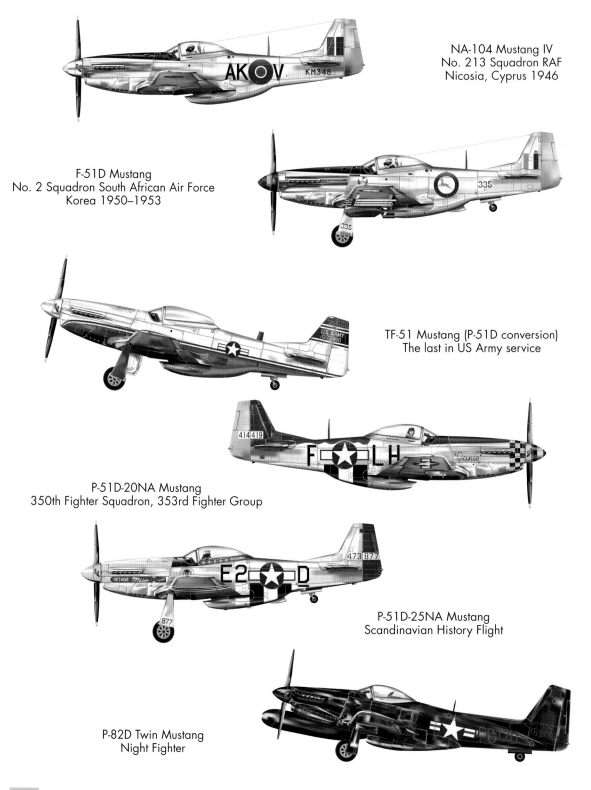

NA-104 Mustang IV
No. 213 Squadron RAF
Nicosia, Cyprus 1946

F-51D Mustang
No. 2 Squadron South African Air Force
Korea 1950–1953

TF-51 Mustang (P-51D conversion)
The last in US Army service

P-51D-20NA Mustang
350th Fighter Squadron, 353rd Fighter Group

P-51D-25NA Mustang
Scandinavian History Flight

P-82D Twin Mustang
Night Fighter

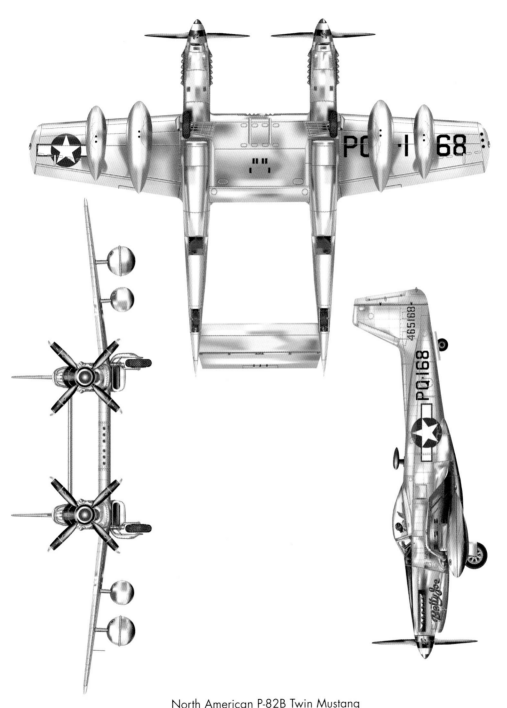

North American P-82B Twin Mustang
Long Range Escort Fighter
'Betty Joe'
Honolulu–New York, non-stop in 14 hours 32 mins, 14 February 1947.
Longest unrefuelled flight by a piston-engined aircraft

A flight of F-82E Twin Mustangs in post-war markings are caught on camera flying in an echelon formation. The F-82E was an Allison-engined version of the Mustang ordered in 1946 as a long-range escort fighter for the newly formed Strategic Air Command. The prominent sway-braces attaching the underwing tank to the wing were necessary to cope with the heavy fuel loads long-range missions called for. (Real Wings Photographs)

## Trials airframes

Throughout the Mustang programme standard airframes were diverted for various development trials. Initially the P-51B was the main test airframe, some being used by NACA to trial various wing sections, as it was the fastest aircraft available at the time. Other trials involved the use of a P-51B for the development of reconnaissance systems, which involved festooning the airframe with various lumps and bumps to house the cameras, and pods under the wings for other camera installations and flares. Initial trials were also carried out to test the bazooka anti-tank weapon as an underwing store. After flight trials in the United States the weapon was deployed in a triple tube format, mainly to units in the Far East.

Once the P-51D was available it too became a trials vehicle. One of the first series of tests that the 'D' model was employed upon was to confirm that all the weapons cleared for the earlier versions could still be used on the P-51D/K aircraft. When the United States became embroiled in the Korean War at least one P-51D was employed on the testing of enlarged long-range fuel tanks, although they were not a normal fit on combat aircraft. In the civilian field a P-51B known as 'Beguine' had a pair of Garrett AIResearch turbojets fitted to each wingtip in a bid to increase the type's top speed. The purpose of this unique installation was to raise the Mustang's top speed in short bursts whilst taking part in the nascent Cleveland air races. Unfortunately the aircraft went out of control and crashed, causing the cancellation of the 1949 meeting.

Across the Atlantic further development work was concentrated on engines and weapons. The first major British programme was of course the prototype installation of a Rolls-Royce Merlin on the front bulkhead of a P-51A Mustang. Unlike the later production versions the trials aircraft had an external intake under the engine, as the cooling system had not been plumbed in. Weapons trials

46-415 PQ-415 was a standard P-82F manufactured for the fighter role. Its wing armament in the centre section was retained, firing over the large pod which contained the APS-4 radar system. The type's armament could be added to by further stores on the outer pylons. F-82s continued in front-line service until the mid 1950s when they were replaced by Northrop F-89 Scorpion jet fighters. *(C P Russell Smith Collection)*

involved using a Mustang Mk I for testing the underwing pod installations of the Vickers-designed 'S' gun, which was a large-calibre cannon designed for anti-tank work.

## Overseas production

Mustang production also moved overseas with a manufacturing line being established in Australia under the control of the CAC. Initially Australia had received American-built P-51Ds and P-51Ks. Designated the CA-17 Mustang Mk 20, the Australian-built airframe was powered by the Packard-built V-1650-3, of which 80 were built from kits. A further 14 were built as the Mk 22 reconnaissance version. A further 40 were manufactured in two batches, being designated the CA-18 Mustang Mk 21. A final batch of 66 were constructed as the Mk 23, this variant having the Rolls-Royce Merlin installed instead of the American engine. Eventually some 200 airframes were constructed in Australia.

Possibly the most unusual expression of the designer's art has to be North American Aviation's answer to a pressing need tendered by the USAAF for a long-range multi-crew night fighter for use over the Pacific Ocean. Instead of returning to the drawing board to create something new, the design department at Inglewood decided to draw upon materials and data already to hand. The proposal submitted to the Army featured two Mustang fuselages joined together using a completely new centre section and tailplane, although the outer wing panels and many of the other systems and components would come from the normal production lines. To their new baby NAA gave the designation NA-120 whilst the USAAF, liking what it saw, designated the type the XP-82. Contract AC-2029 was issued on 7 January 1944 to cover the building of two prototypes.

The specified powerplants for the XP-82 were a pair of Packard-built Merlins designated V-1650-23/25. These were handed units as the designation shows – one propeller would turn in a clockwise direction whilst the other rotated in the opposite manner. This set-up would virtually eliminate any torque. Experience had shown that such an effect was an unacceptable hazard, as the saga of the P-38 Lightnings built for the RAF had revealed.

The fuselages that the engines were bolted onto bore a superficial resemblance to the single-seaters, but in reality they were a complete redesign. Not only were they longer, but they also had completely new mounting points for other major airframe assemblies. Armament too changed its location. Whereas the day fighters spread their internal weaponry across both wings, that of the XP-82 was concentrated in the new centre section although the outer wing panels were capable of carrying external armament and fuel tanks. The main gear attachment points no longer sat in the wing panels as they had been relocated to the wing roots, although both legs still retracted inwards. As there were two fuselages it seemed natural to retain a retractable tailwheel for each although there was a short period spent toying with the idea of a single unit located in the central tailplane. This had quickly been dropped on the grounds of fragility and the disturbance that such a protrusion would cause to the aerodynamics.

## XP-82 maiden flight

Assembly of the new fighter prototype proceeded apace. The first XP-82 was ready for its maiden flight on 15 April 1945, being piloted from Inglewood by NAA Chief Test Pilot Bob Chilton. Such was the excellent behaviour of the aircraft on this first flight that the USAAF immediately confirmed the provisional order that had been placed in March 1944 for 500 machines. A further two prototypes were also placed on contract with the third machine being designated the XP-82A. This would differ from its siblings in that the powerplants would be changed to the Allison V-1710-119 engine as an insurance should Britain decide to cancel the licence for production of the Rolls-Royce Merlin at the end of the war.

The first variant would be the P-82B, company designation NA-123 but by now known familiarly as the Twin Mustang. Differences from the prototypes included the capability to carry four 1,000 lb bombs on the outer wings, two per side. Fittings were added to allow the carriage of a large gun pod with eight machine-guns plus ammunition, in addition to the six weapons already in place in the centre section.

## Wartime contracts slashed

North American began to set up the production line on confirmation of the contract and was ready to start deliveries when the Atom bombs were dropped on Japan. This sudden and cataclysmic end to the war also saw a massive cancelling of orders. The contract for 500 aircraft was quickly dropped to twenty. At this point the P-82 saga could have ended, but the USAAF was in need of a long-range high-performance night fighter to replace the Northrop P-61 Black Widow. Thus the NAA product underwent a transformation from heavyweight all-purpose fighter to a stalker in the night skies. To expedite this process the tenth and eleventh production P-82Bs were selected to act as development machines. Designated the P-82C and P-82D respectively, the airframes were identical, the primary difference being in the radar each machine carried. The P-82C carried the SCR720 array whilst the P-82D used the APS-4. To fit in with their new role both aircraft were repainted in a gloss black overall scheme. The right-hand fuselage cockpit, which had originally been fitted with a full set of flight controls, was refitted with the controls and displays needed in the interceptor role whilst the aerials for the radar were carried about the outer wing panels.

## Twin Mustang record-breaker

Meanwhile all bar one of the production P-82Bs were leading a quiet existence. The exception was airframe 44-65168, which was fitted with extra fuel tanks behind the cockpits and sported four huge 310-gallon tanks under the outer wings. The aircraft was used to evaluate the P-82 on long-distance flight, but the primary purpose of the programme was to determine the effects of long-duration flights on aircrew. Named 'Betty Jo', after the senior pilot's wife, the aircraft departed Hickam Field in Hawaii for New York piloted by Lieutenant-Colonel R E Thacker and Lieutenant John Ard.

The mounting point under the wing centre section on the P-82 was a convenient place for mounting stores, and both North American and the USAF tried out different podded systems on the big fighter. This particular pod contains a reconnaissance set-up with a selection of cameras for taking oblique and vertical photos. Other pod types built for the Twin Mustang contained machine-guns and ammunition. *(NAA Archive)*

The flight, which covered 5,051 miles and lasted 14 hours and 33 minutes, was undertaken on 27 February 1947. Average speed for the trip had been 334 mph, which would have been higher had the external tanks been jettisoned. As it was, they remained attached, thus slowing the aircraft down and causing minor stability problems.

Trials and evaluation of both versions of the night fighter revealed an outstanding aircraft that was blessed with speed and manoeuvrability, even with drag-inducing radar antennas. A variety of Twin Mustangs were manufactured to cover numerous roles.

The Model NA-144 appeared as the Allison-powered P-82E, of which 100 were delivered for the day-fighter role. The subsequent P-82F was also Allison-powered and was intended for the night-fighter role, for which purpose the APS-4 radar was installed. 100 of this variant were constructed. The final Twin Mustang was the P-82G, which numbered 50 in total. This was another night-fighter version, equipped with the SCR720 radar whose antenna and valve electronics were mounted in a huge pod carried under the wing centre section. Production of the Twin Mustang began in 1946 and would continue until March 1949, when the final P-82G was delivered from the Inglewood production line.

Given the post-war rundown of the American forces, the Twin Mustang would normally have had a relatively short period in front-line service. But the Korean War erupted in 1950. The first airframes thrown into the fray were those F-82s that were stationed in the region as part of the Far East Air Force. In fact the credit for the first combat kill of the war was given to a Twin Mustang crew. Although designed as a night fighter, the F-82s gave a creditable account of themselves as day fighters in the ground-attack role. With radar pods removed the aircraft carried out raids on North Korean forces, dumps and other strategic targets before returning to their designed role when other types became available.

Although they had performed well, the F-82s were not really suited to front-line action, and so once more modern machines were available the remaining F-82G Twin Mustangs were withdrawn and passed to Alaskan Air Command. After winterisation the remaining machines entered service as the F-82H. Their service life was short, since they were quickly withdrawn as spares shortages became critical.

## Twin Mustang specification

The specifications for the P-82 are: Span 51ft 3in; Length 38ft 1in; Height 13ft; Wing area 408 sq ft.

Empty weight 13,405 lb; Loaded weight 22,000 lb.

Max speed 482 mph; Cruise speed 227 mph; Max ceiling 41,600 ft; Rate of climb 3,500 ft/min; Max range 1,400 miles.

Powerplants: two Packard V-1650-23/25 rated at 1,860 hp each.

Armament: six 0.50 inch machine-guns in wing centre section with four outer wing pylons for a variety of weapons.

The final disappearance of the Mustang from USAF and ANG service in 1957 released hundreds of surplus P-51s onto the civilian market. The rights to the Mustang design were then purchased from North American Aircraft by the Cavalier Aircraft Corporation, which attempted to market the surplus Mustang aircraft throughout the US and potential overseas markets. In 1967 and again in 1972 the

USAF procured additional batches of Mustangs from Cavalier, most of them destined for air forces in South America and Asia that were participating in the Military Assistance Program.

These aircraft were remanufactured from existing F-51D airframes but were fitted with new V-1650-7 engines, a new radio fit, the taller F-51H type fin and rudder, and a stronger wing which could carry six 0.50 inch machine-guns and a total of eight underwing hardpoints. Two 1,000 lb bombs and six 5-inch rockets could be carried. They all had the original F-51D-style canopy, but carried a second seat for an observer behind the pilot. Although these new Mustangs were intended for delivery to South American and Asian nations through the MAP, they were delivered with full USAF markings and were allocated new serial numbers (67-14862/14866, 67-22579/22582 and 72-1526/1541). One additional Mustang was a two-seat dual-control TF-51D (67-14866) with an enlarged canopy and only four wing guns.

## Helicopter chase plane

During 1968 the United States Army used a retired F-51D, 44-72990, as a chase aircraft for the Lockheed YAH-56 Cheyenne armed helicopter project. This aircraft was so successful that the Army ordered two further F-51Ds from Cavalier in 1968 for use at Fort Rucker as chase planes. They were assigned the serials 68-15795 and 68-15796. These airframes had wingtip fuel tanks and were operated unarmed. Following the end of the Cheyenne programme both aircraft were employed on other projects. One of them, 68-15795, was later fitted with a 106-mm recoilless rifle for evaluation of the weapon's value in attacking fortified ground targets. Although reasonably successful the weapon was not adopted for service use.

There was one final fling to extend the life of the Mustang as a front-line aircraft. It was intended for use in countries that had neither the money nor the infrastructure to support a more advanced type. The pioneer of this programme was the Cavalier Aircraft Corporation, based in Florida, a company that had already worked wonders with refurbishing weary examples of the F-51 for various users.

Now on display at Fort Rucker, home of the US Army aviation museum, this F-51D had been partially remanufactured by Cavalier to extend its operational life. Whilst in use as a chase plane the Mustang gained a white painted portion to the upper canopy to help reflect the heat. *(Real Wings Photographs)*

Designated the Cavalier Turbo Mustang III, its main altered feature was the installation of a Rolls-Royce Dart Mk 510 turboprop powerplant rated at 1,740 shp, although the CEO of Cavalier, David Lindsay, had originally schemed the installation of a Lycoming T-55 engine. The airframe the engine was mounted on was not the usual reworked item, but one that had been newly built from unused major assemblies with any minor items being manufactured as required. In 1968 Cavalier flight-tested the aircraft as the Turbo-Mustang III, civilian registered as N6167U.

Under the skin there were further changes from the veteran of World War Two, especially in the area of avionics. Major revisions saw the deletion of the old-type radios and their replacement by more modern equipment. The complete suite consisted of an ARN 52 TACAN, ARN 80 ILS/VOR, AN/ARQ 50 UHF/ADF, ARC 109 UHF/AM, ARC 114 UHF/FM, ARC 115 VHF/AM, ARC 123 HF/SSB and a KY 28 which was a security and IFF transponder. The armament capability was also increased, courtesy of the beefed-up wing structure, and was carried on six pylons. The inboard pylons were rated at 1,000 lb each whilst the outers had a rating of 750 lb each. Typical weapons cleared for use included the SUU-7A bomblet dispenser, BLU-1/B and 11/B fire bombs plus a variety of bombs, rockets and gunpods.

## Turbine power

Although the Turbo Mustang was technically successful, the lack of sales saw the Cavalier company deciding to sell the development rights to the Piper Aircraft Corporation, and cancelling any further work on the re-engined Mustang project. On 4 November 1970 the Dart-powered Mustang prototype was delivered to the Piper factory at Vero Beach.

During this period the United States was heavily engaged in the Vietnam War and combat experience indicated that there was a need for a low-cost, high-performance close support aircraft for use by foreign air forces in receipt of MAP assistance. This project was given the name 'Pave Coin'. In pursuit of production contracts under the *Pave Coin* programme the Piper company undertook a more ambitious Mustang conversion effort. One single-seat F-51D and one two-seat TF-51D

The Piper PA-48 Enforcer was the last development of the Mustang. Only two were built and, although they would have been highly versatile and effective in the counter-insurgency role, no orders would be forthcoming. The days of the Mustang in combat had ended, four decades after its first flight. (Real Wings Photographs)

airframe were fitted with the 2,455 shp Lycoming T55-L-9 turboprop engine. The project was given the name 'Enforcer' by Piper, and the first aircraft flew on 19 April 1971. Later that year the USAF evaluated an Enforcer prototype and confirmed the original performance claims, but overall showed very little enthusiasm for the project.

## The last Mustangs

Even though the USAF failed to see any use for the Enforcer, congressional pressure led eventually to a contract being placed in September 1981 for Piper to construct two new prototypes for evaluation. They were to be known under the company designation of PA-48. The two PA-48 prototypes were given civilian registrations rather than military serial numbers and were never given any formal military designations.

The PA-48 Enforcer bore only the slightest resemblance to the earlier F-51D, with only ten per cent of the parts being common to both. The fuselage was lengthened by 19 inches aft of the wing and larger tail surfaces were fitted to increase longitudinal stability. Power was

provided by a Lycoming T55-L-9 turboprop. The familiar trademark Mustang ventral scoop was completely removed, and a large turboprop exhaust was fitted on the left-hand side of the fuselage just ahead of the cockpit. A Yankee rocket ejector seat was fitted in the single-seat cockpit. Provisions for wingtip tanks were made and ten underwing hardpoints were fitted. The fixed wing-mounted guns were removed, and all gun armament was carried in underwing pods.

The two PA-48s first flew on 9 April and 8 July 1983 respectively with the USAF conducting its evaluations at Eglin AFB and Edwards AFB during 1983–4. Gross weight was 14,000 lb. Maximum speed was 403 mph and cruising speed was 363 mph. Service ceiling was 37,600 feet and combat radius with two gun pods was 469 miles. The PA-48 Enforcer was unsuccessful in obtaining any production orders, and both prototypes were put in storage by the USAF in late 1986. One of them, N481PE, is now on display in Dayton, Ohio, in the annexe building of the USAF museum at Wright Patterson AFB.

# Appendix 1
# Weapons and Systems

**P-51A/Mustang Mk I:** Pair of 0.50-calibre machine guns in the lower nose section plus a pair of similar weapons mounted in each wing. Four 0.30-calibre weapons were superimposed above the heavier machine-guns in the wing. Access to the wing guns was through a series of panels in the upper wing surfaces. Each gun with 1,260 rounds in purpose-built armament tanks. Wing guns were originally canted slightly, causing problems. Pointing slightly upwards, certain manoeuvres would cause the guns to jam. Field modification programme to re-align the machine guns cured problem. Deletion of nose guns later reduced weight and cut back on maintenance requirements.

**A-36A Apache:** Additional ground attack capacity for use in the dive-bombing role. 500-lb bombs carried on underwing streamlined pylons, one per wing.

**Mk IA:** Interim upgraded version of the Mustang I for RAF, armed with four 20-mm cannons in the wings.

**P-51B/P-51C/Mustang III:** Standard armament set-up of four or six 0.50-in machine guns in the wings, each with 1,260 rounds of ammunition each. Underwing pylon fit upgraded to carry 1,000-lb bombs. On all versions the bombs could be released in level flight, in a dive or at an angle of up to thirty degrees in an upwards direction.

**Extra fuel:** In addition to electrical weapons-release system, underwing pylons were also plumbed for fuel tank carriage. Two connections built into each pylon: fuel feed line and a pneumatic feed that pressurised the tank. This last forced fuel into the main system. Tanks were attached via sway braces and fore and aft locating lugs. On long sorties tanks were jettisoned as they emptied or to clean up the airframe for combat. Release was mechanical in nature and could be operated under any circumstances including emergencies. A single fuel tank could be fitted to counterbalance a weapon on the opposite side, although both unused fuel tank lines required blanking.

**Drop tanks:** Tens of thousands were manufactured. Majority used in combat were made of aluminium, though later tanks were made from highly compressed paper.

No Mustang ever carried stores on the centreline. The main reason was that the airflow dynamics for radiator cooling intake would have been disturbed, making the fighter less efficient. In any case, the airframe design left little space for pylons or shackles, since the inner edges of the undercarriage bays were separated only by a centre supporting beam, leaving no room for a pylon.

**Anti-tank:** Mustangs were fitted with Bazooka-type tube-launched anti-tank launchers. Initially tested as a singleton and proved surprisingly effective at destroying ground targets. Production version incorporated three Bazookas clustered together for an even more effective assault weapon. Eighth and Ninth Air Forces in Britain and 15th AF in Italy, primarily escort

forces, did not use many. Used extensively in the China-Burma-India theatre, however, where Mustangs were more often used in direct support of ground forces.

**Napalm:** An incendiary petroleum mix which became a standard Mustang weapon. Initially modified fuel tanks, which had a tendency to tumble uncontrollably. More aerodynamic tanks controllable during aiming and release were developed. Highly successful as a 'Bunker-buster' in Korea.

**P-51D/Mustang IV:** Already cleared for most of the weaponry available when first introduced. Further armaments under development including the 5-inch high-velocity rocket, fitted with a 60-lb war head. Launch mountings installed under outer wing panels, allowing a maximum of four per wing. Greatest successes in Korea, used to great effect by F-51s of both USAF and the SAAF.

**Gunsights:** Primary gunsights installed in the Mustang included the N-9 and K-14A units. The N-9 was the old-type aiming ring with a smaller 'pipper' in the centre. The K-14A was of the illuminated reticule type with setable offsets to allow for different gun setup angles and was a licence-built British gyro sight. Once mastered, it proved extremely effective.

**Camera gun:** Mounted in port wing root, coupled to gunsight and operated by the firing button. Used for recording and confirming kills and weapons accuracy. Calibration and harmonisation plus gun convergence angles could be adjusted on the ground using a special sight-line level indicator. Mustang raised on jacks and trestles in gun testing area, and then trimmed to represent level flight. Sighting board assembled in front of the aircraft, allowing sight reticule to be set via the indicator against a target mark on the board. Guns were then test-fired to check the alignment.

**F-6 Mustang:** Oblique camera offset to the port side. Three sight marks engraved into canopy, aligned with marks painted onto three equidistant points on the left wing. Using the six marks allowed oblique cameras with offsets of between 9 and 30 degrees to be catered for.

**P-82 Twin Mustang:** Long-range fighter could carry the same weapons load as its single-seater sibling, with machine-guns concentrated in the newly developed wing centre section. Centre section also had mountings for a variety of pods, including rockets, cannon, machine-guns, reconnaissance, and radar for night-fighter variants.

**Mustang rebuilds:** Cavalier Turbo Mustang and Piper Enforcer featured strengthened structure. Able to carry much of the tactical armament available in the USAF inventory of the 1960s. This included rocket pods, 'Willie Pete' white phosphorous target markers, bombs up to 1,000 lb in weight and napalm tanks. Plumbing was also available for extra external fuel tanks.

# Appendix 2
# Mustang Production

The P-51 Mustang was produced at two North American Aviation facilities.
Those manufactured at the Inglewood, California plant had the suffix NA added to their model numbers. The second facility located at Dallas, Texas, to increase production of the fighter, had the suffix -NT added to its model numbers.

| Model No | Designation | Registration | Qty | Construction no |
|---|---|---|---|---|
| NA-73X | NA-73X | NX19998 | 1 | 73-3097 |
| NA-73 | XP-51-NA | 41-38 41-39 | 2 | 73-3101 73-3107 |
| NA-91 | P-51A-NA | 41-37320 to 37469 | 150 | 91-11981 to 12130 |
| NA-99 | P-51A-1NA | 43-6003 to 6102 | 100 | 99-22106 to 22205 |
| NA-99 | P-51A-5NA | 43-6013 to 6157 | 55 | 99-22206 to 22260 |
| NA-99 | P-51A-10NA | 43-6158 to 6312 | 155 | 99-22261 to 22415 |
| NA-101 | XP-51B-NA | 41-37352/41-37421 | 2 | converted from P-51-NA |
| NA-102 | P-51B-1NA | 43-12093 to 12492 | 400 | 102-24541 to 24940 |
| NA-104 | P-51B-5NA | 43-6313 to 6352 | 800 | 104-22816 to 23305, |
| | | 43-6353 to 6752 | | 24431 to 24540, |
| | | 43-6753 to 7112 | | 24941 to 25140 |
| NA-104 | P-51B-10NA | 43-7111 to 7202 | 398 | 104-25141 to 25230 |
| | | 42-106429 to 106538 | | |
| | | 42-106541 to 106738 | | |
| NA-104 | P-51B-15NA | 42-106739 to 106908 | 390 | 104-25541 to 25780 |
| | | 42-106909 to 106978 | | |
| | | 43-24752 to 24901 | | 104-25781 to 25930 |
| NA-103 | P-51C-1NT | 42-102979 to 103328 | 350 | 103-22416 to 22765 |
| NA-103 | P-51C-5NT | 42-103329 to 103778 | 50 | 103-22766 to 22815 |
| | | | | 103-25933 to 26332 |
| NA-103 | P-51C-10NT | 42-103779 to 103978 | 950 | 103-26333 to 26532 |
| | | 43-24902 to 25251 | | 103-26533 to 26882 |
| | | 44-10753 to 10782 | 400 | 111-28886 to 28915 |
| NA-111 | P-51C-11NT | 44-10783 to 10817 | | 111-28916 to 28950 |
| NA-111 | P-51C-10NT | 44-10818 to 10852 | | 111-28951 to 28985 |
| NA-111 | P-51C-11NT | 44-10853 to 10858 | | 111-28986 to 28991 |
| NA-111 | P-51C-10NT | 44-10859 to 11036 | | 111-28992 to 29169 |
| NA-111 | P-51C-11NT | 44-11037 to 11122 | | 111-29170 to 29255 |
| NA-111 | P-51C-10NT | 44-11123 to 11152 | | 111-29256 to 29285 |
| NA-111 | P-51D-5NT | 44-11153 to 11352 | | 111-29286 to 29485 |
| NA-106 | XP-51D-NA | 42-106539 to 106540 | 2 | converted from P-51B-1NA |
| NA-109 | P-51D-5NA | 44-13253 to 14052 | 800 | 109-27686 to 28485 |

| Model No | Designation | Registration | Qty | Construction no |
|---|---|---|---|---|
| NA-109 | P-51D-10NA | 44-14053 to 14852 | | |
| NA-109 | P-51D-15NA | 44-14853 to 15252 | 900 | 109-28486 to 28885 |
| | | 44-15253 to 15752 | | 35536 to 36035 |
| NA-122 | P-51D-20NA | 44-63160 to 64159 | 1600 | 122-38006 to 31885 |
| | | 44-72027 to 72126 | | 122-31886 to 31985, |
| | | 44-72127 to 72626 | | 38586 to 39085 |
| NA-122 | P-51D-25NA | 44-72627 to 73626 | 1600 | 122-39086 to 40085, |
| | | 44-73627 to 74226 | | 40167 to 40766 |
| NA-122 | P-51D-30NA | 44-74227 to 75026 | 800 | 122-40767 to 41566 |
| NA-111 | P-51D-5NT | 44-11153 to 11352 | 200 | |
| NA-111 | P-51D-20NT | 44-12853 to 13252 | 400 | 111-30686 to 30885, |
| | | | | 111-36036 to 36135 |
| | | | | 109-26886 to 27685 |
| NA-124 | P-51D-25NT | 44-84390 to 84989 | 600 | 120-43744 to 43745 |
| | | 45-11343 to11542 | | 124-48096 to 48295 |
| NA-124 | P-51D-30NT | 45-11543 to 11742 | | 124-48296 to 48495 |
| TP-51D | | 45-11443 to 11450 | 10 | |
| | | 44-84610 to 84611 | | |
| NA-105 | XP-51F-NA | 43-43332 to 43334 | 3 | |
| NA-195 | XP-51G-NA | 43-43335 to 43336 | 2 | |
| NA-126 | P-51H-1NA | 44-64160 to 64179 | 555 | 126-37586 to 37605 |
| NA-126 | P-51H-5NA | 44-64180 to 64459 | | 126-37606 to 37885 |
| NA-126 | P-51H-10NA | 44-64460 to 64714 | | 126-37886 to 38140. |
| NA-126 | P-51H-NA | 44-64715 to 65159 | cancelled contract | |
| NA-105 | XP-51J-NA | 44-76027 44-76028 | 2 | |
| NA-111 | P-51K-1NT | 44-11353 to 11552 | 200 | 111-29486 to 29685 |
| NA-111 | P-51K-5NT | 44-11553 to 11952 | 400 | 111-29686 to 30085 |
| NA-111 | P-51K-10NT | 44-11953 to 12752 | 600 | 111-30086 to 30685. |
| NA-111 | P-51K-15NT | 44-12553 to 12852 | | 111-30686 to 30885, |
| | | | | 111-36036 to 36135 to RAAF |
| NA-xxx | P-51L-NT | 44-91004 to 92003 | cancelled contract | |
| NA-124 | P-51M-NT | 45-11743 | 1 | |

| Model No | Designation | Registration | Qty | Construction no |
|---|---|---|---|---|
| **A-36 Apache** | | | | |
| NA-97 | A-36A | 42-83663 to 84162 | 500 | 97-15881 to 16380 |

| Model No | Designation | Registration | Qty | Construction no |
|---|---|---|---|---|
| **Reconnaissance Mustangs** | | | | |
| Conversion | F-6K-5NT | 44-11554, | 56 | |
| | | 44-11897 to 44-11951 | | |
| Conversion | F-6K-10NT | 44-11993 to 44-12008 | 63 | |
| | | 44-12216 to 44-12237 | | |
| | | 44-12459 to 44-12471 | | |
| | | 44-12523 to 44-12534 | | |
| Conversion | F-6K-15NT | 44-12810 to 44-12852 | 43 | |
| Conversion | F-6D-20NT | 44-13020 to 44-13039 | 31 | |
| | | 44-13131 to 44-13140 | | |
| | | 44-13181 | | |
| Conversion | F-6D-25NT | 44-84509 to 44-84540 | 70 | |
| | | 44-84566 | | |
| | | 44-84773 to 44-84778 | | |
| | | 44-84835 to 44-84855 | | |

| Model No | Designation | Registration | Qty | Construction no |
|---|---|---|---|---|
| **British Mustangs** | | | | |
| NA-73 | Mustang Mk I | AG345 to AG664 | 320 | |
| NA-83 | | AL958 to AM257 | | |
| | | AP164 to AP263 | 300 | |
| NA-99 | Mustang Mk IA | FD418 to FD567 | 150 | |
| NA-99 | Mustang Mk II | FR890 to FR939 | 50 | |
| NA-104/111 | Mustang Mk III | FB100 to FB339 | 300 | |
| | Mustang Mk III | FR411 | 1 | evaluation aircraft |
| NA-104/111 | | FX848 to FZ197 | 250 | |
| NA104 | | HB821 to HB961 | 141 | |
| | | HK944 to HK947 | 3 | ex-USAAF |
| | | HK955 to HK956 | 3 | ex-USAAF |
| | | KH421 to KH640 | 450 | includes (i) & (ii) |
| | | SR406 to SR440 | 34 | ex-USAAF |
| | Mustang Mk IV | KH641 to KH670 | (i) | |
| | Mustang Mk IVA | KH671 to KH870 | (ii) | |
| | | KM100 to KM492 | 700 | includes (iii) |
| | | TK586 | 1 | trials aircraft |
| | | TK589 | 1 | trials aircraft |
| | | KM744 to KM799 | (iii) | cancelled contract |
| | XP-51G | FR410 | 1 | |

| Model No | Designation | Registration | Qty | Construction no |
|---|---|---|---|---|
| | Mustang Mk V | FR409 | 1 | XP-51F redesignated |
| | A-36A | EW998 | 1 | |
| **Australian Mustangs** | | | | |
| NA-105 | CA-17 Mk 20 | A68-1 to 80 | 80 | |
| NA-105 | CA-18 Mk 21 | A68-81 to 106 | 26 | |
| NA-105 | CA-18 Mk 22 | A68-107 to120 | 14 | |
| NA-105 | CA-18 Mk 22 | A68-187 to 200 | 14 | |
| NA-105 | CA-18 Mk 23 | A68-121 to 186 | 66 | |

| Model No | Designation | Registration | Qty | Construction no |
|---|---|---|---|---|
| **Rebuilds and conversions** | | | | |
| F-51D | | 67-14862 to 14865 | 4 | Cavalier rebuild/conversion |
| F-51D | | 67-22579 to 22582 | 4 | Cavalier rebuild/conversion |
| F-51D | | 68-15795 to 15796 | 2 | Cavalier rebuild/conversion |
| F-51D | | 72-1536 to 1541 | 6 | Cavalier rebuild/conversion |
| TF-51D | | 67-14886 | 1 | Cavalier rebuild/conversion |
| Turboprop | | N201PE N202PE | 2 | Cavalier rebuild/conversion |

| Model No | Designation | Registration | Qty | Construction no |
|---|---|---|---|---|
| **Twin Mustangs** | | | | |
| NA-120 | XP-82-NA | 44-83886 to 83887 | 2 | 120-43742 to 43743 |
| NA-121 | XP-82A-NA | 44-83888 to 83889 | 1 | 120-43744 to 43745 |
| NA-123 | P-82B-NA | 44-65160 to 65168 | 9 | 123-43746 to 43754 |
| NA-122 | P-82C-NA | 44-65169 | 1 | 123-43755 |
| NA-124 | P-82D-NA | 44-65170 | 1 | 123-43756 |
| NA-123 | P-82B-NA | 44-65171 to 65179 | 9 | 123-43757 to 43765 |
| NA-144 | P-82E-NA | 46-255 to 354 | 100 | 144-38141 to 38240 |
| | | redesignated to F-82E in 1948 | | |
| NA-150 | P-52G-NA | 46-355 to 383 | 29 | 150-38241 to 38269 |
| | | redesignated to F-82G in 1948 | | |
| NA-151 | P-82H-NA | 46-384 to 388 | 5 | 150-38270 to 38274 |
| | | redesignated to F-82G in 1948 | | |
| NA-150 | P-82G-NA | 46-389 to 404 | 16 | 150-38275 to 38290 |
| | | redesignated to F-82G in1948 | | |
| NA-149 | P-82F-NA | 46-405 to 495 | 19 | 149-38291 to 38381 |
| | | redesignated to F-82F in 1948 | | |
| NA-151 | P-82H-NA | 46-496 to 504 | 9 | 150-38382 to 38390 |
| | | redesignated to F-82H in 1948 | | |

| | |
|---|---|
| **Total single-fuselage Mustangs** | **15,705** |
| **Total Twin Mustangs** | **202** |
| **Overall Mustang total** | **15,907** |

# Appendix 3
# Mustang Survivors

Only a small percentage of the thousands of Mustangs built survive, though that small number is probably greater than any other warbird. There are, at the last count, 275 extant P-51s throughout the world. Of these there are 154 currently registered for flying whilst another 51 are preserved in museums and collections on static display. A further 46 are undergoing rebuild to flying status whilst another 20 are stored awaiting a decision. To complete the picture there are 4 for which there is no final fate. Listed below are most of the currently flyable airframes together with many of those being restored.

| Civil Reg. | Military serial | Name | P-51 type | Owner/operator | Current base | Status |
|---|---|---|---|---|---|---|
| N51NA | 41-038 | | XP-51 | Experimental Aircraft Assoc | Oshkosh WI | Display |
| N39502 | 42-83665 | 'Margie H' | A-36A | USAF Museum | Dayton OH | Display |
| N251A | 42-83731 | | A-36A | Lone Star Museum | Texas | Flyable |
| N4067V | 42-83738 | | A-36A | John Paul | Caldwell ID | Restore |
| N/A | 43-43335 | 'Marjorie Hart' | XP-51G | John Morgan | La Canada CA | Restore |
| N51Z | 43-6006 | 'Polar Bear' | P-51A-1NA | Jerry Gabe | Hollister CA | Flyable |
| N4235Y | 43-6251 | | P-51A-10NA | Planes of Fame Museum | Valle AZ | Flyable |
| N90358 | 43-6274 | | P-51A-10NA | Charles Nichols | Chino CA | Flyable |
| Nl61429 | 42-103645 | 'Tuskegee Airman' | P-51C-10NT | Confederate Air Force | St Paul MN | Flyable |
| N1204 | 42-103831 | 'Ina, the Macon Belle' | P-51C-10NT | Kermit Weeks | Tamiami FL | Flyable |
| G-PSIC | 43-25147 | 'Princess Elizabeth' | P-51C-10NT | Stephen Grey | Britain | Flyable |
| N405HC | 44-10753 | 'Its about time' | P-51-Cavalier | Heber Costello | Oak Grove LA | Flyable |
| N451TB | 44-11153 | | P-51D-5NT | Anthony Banta | Dover DE | Restore |
| N31RK | 44-13009 | | P-51D-20NT | Richard Knowlton | Portland OR | Restore |
| N5551D | 44-13016 | 'Dove of Peace' | P-51D-20NT | Calvin Burgess | Bethany OK | Flyable |
| N71FT | 44-13105 | 'Strega' | P-51D-20NT | Bill Destefani | Shafter CA | Flyable |
| N51DL | 44-13257 | | P-51D-5NA | Lindair Inc | Sarasota FL | Flyable |
| N/A | 44-13954 | 'Da Quake' | P-51D-10NA | David Kingshot | Britain | Restore |
| N51TK | 44-63350 | 'Lou IV' | P-51D-20NA | Charles Greenhill | Kenosha WS | Flyable |
| N63476 | 44-63476 | 'City of Winnepeg' | P-51D-20NA | Bob May | Nth Dakota | Flyable |
| N51EA | 44-63507/ | 'Double Trouble Two' | P-51D-20NA | Max Vogelsang | Switzerland | Flyable |
| | 72483 | | | | | |
| N51HR | 44-63542 | 'Sizzlin Liz' | P-51D-20NA | Ted Contri | Carson City NV | Flyable |
| N51DH | 44-63567 | | P-51D-20NA | Sproose Goose Museum | McMinnville OR | Flyable |
| N151JT | 44-63577 | | P-51D-20NA | John Turgyan | New Egypt NJ | Restore |
| N51ES | 44-63634 | 'Big Beautiful Doll' | P-51D-20NA | Ed Shipley | Malvern PA | Flyable |
| N5500S | 44-63655/44-74543 | | P-51D-20NA | AMBHIB Inc | Kenosha WS | Flyable |
| N41749 | 44-63663 | 'Miss Marylin II' | P-51D-20NA | Richard Hanson | Batavia IL | Flyable |
| N1751D | 44-63675 | 'Sierra Sue/ Gul Kalle' | P-51D-20NA | Roger Christgau | Eden Prairie MN | Flyable |
| N26PW | 44-63701 | 'Grim Reaper' | P-51D-20NA | Sal Rubino Jr | Merced CA | Flyable |
| N20MS | 44-63807 | | P-51D-20NA | Jon Vesely | Inverness IL | Restore |
| N451BC | 44-63810 | 'Angels Playmate' | P-51D-20NA | Joe Newsome | Cheraw SC | Flyable |
| SE-BKG | 44-63864 | 'Yellow K' | P-51D-20NA | Leif Jaraker | Vasteras Sweden | Flyable |
| N151TF | 44-63865 | | P-51D-20NA | Classic American Aircraft | Chino CA | Restore |
| CF-FUZ | 44-63889 | | P-51D-20NA | Gary McCann | Canada | Flyable |
| N3333E | 44-63893 | 'Dixie' | P-51D-20NA | Wayne Rudd | Colorado | Flyable |

| Civil Reg. | Military serial | Name | P-51 type | Owner/operator | Current base | Status |
|---|---|---|---|---|---|---|
| N51CK | 44-64005 | 'Mary Mine' | P-51D-20NA | Charles Kemp | Jackson MS | Flyable |
| N339TH | 44-64122 | 'Kansas City Kitty' | P-51D-20NA | Wes Stricker | Jefferson City MO | Flyable |
| N63407 | 44-63407 | | P-51D-20NA | Connie Edwards | Big Spring TX | Restore |
| G-LYNE | 44-72028 | | P-51D-20NA | Robertson/Anderson | Britain | Restore |
| F-AZMU | 44-72035 | 'Jumpin' Jacques' | P-51D-20NA | Jacques Bourret | St Rambert d 'Albon FR | Flyable |
| N68JR | 44-72051 | 'Sweet Revenge' | P-51D-20NA | Roland Fagen | Granite Falls MN | Flyable |
| N951HB | 44-72059 | | P-51D-20NA | Vintage Aero | Maine | Restore |
| N510JS | 44-72086 | 'Baby Duck' | P-51D-20NA | Joseph Scogna | Yardley PA | Flyable |
| N51PT | 44-72145 | 'Petie 3rd' | P-51D-20NA | Peter McManus | Baltimore MD | Flyable |
| N5460V | 44-72192 | 'Straw Boss 2' | P-51D-20NA | CA Warbirds | Hollister CA | Flyable |
| SAAF 325 | 44-72202 | | P-51D-20NA | S. African AF | S. Africa | Flyable |
| G-BIXL | 44-72216 | 'Miss Helen' | P-51D-20NA | Robert Lamplough | England | Flyable |
| N251JC | 44-72339 | | P-51D-20NA | Cavanaugh Flight Museum | Dallas TX | Flyable |
| N723FH | 44-72364 | | P-51D-20NA | Flying Heritage Collection | Arlington WA | Restore |
| N13Y | 44-72400 | | P-51D-20NA | | Bradley CT | Restore |
| N7551T | 44-72438 | 'Hell-er Bust' | P-51D-20NA | Bob Jepson | Kissimmee FL | Flyable |
| N151DM | 44-72483/ 44-13250 | 'Ridge Runner III' | P-51D-20NA | Dan Martin | Hollister CA | Flyable |
| N44727 | 44-72739 | 'Man O 'War' | P-51D-25NA | Elmer Ward | Chino CA | Flyable |
| G-SUSY | 44-72773 | 'Susy' | P-51D-25NA | Paul Morgan | UK | Flyable |
| N151D | 44-72777 | 'Sparkie' | P-51D-25NA | Steve Sehgetti | Vacaville CA | Flyable |
| N471R | 44-72811 | 'Huntress III' | P-51D-25NA | Robert Converse | Shafter CA | Flyable |
| N51YS | 44-72826 | 'Old Boy' | P-51D-25NA | Steve Collins | Atlanta GA | Flyable |
| N335 | 44-72902 | 'American Dreamer' | P-51D-25NA | Bonzer | Champlin AZ | Restore |
| N41748 | 44-72907 | | P-51D-25NA | Duane Doyle | Hollister CA | Restore |
| N93TF | 44-72922 | 'Scat VII' | P-51D-25NA | Jim Shuttleworth | Huntington IN | Flyable |
| XB-HVL | 44-72934 | 'Shangri-La' | P-51D-25NA | Humberto Lobo | Monterey Mexico | Flyable |
| N7711C | 44-72936 | | P-51D-25NA | Marvin Crouch | Encino CA | Restore |
| N5427V | 44-72942 | 'Petie 2nd' | P-51D-25NA | Anthony Buechler | Waukesha WI | Flyable |
| N51JB | 44-73029 | 'Bald Eagle' | P-51D-25NA | Jim Beasley | Philadelphia PA | Flyable |
| N151BL | 44-73079 | | P-51D-25NA | Bill Dause | Lodi CA | Flyable |
| N5074K | 44-73081 | | P-51D-25NA | Mike Coutches | Hayward CA | Restore |
| N251SQ | 44-73117 | | P-51D-25NA | Square One Aviation | Chino CA | Restore |
| N151SE | 44-73129 | 'Merlin's Magic' | P-51D-25NA | Stu Eberhardt | Livermore/ Hollister CA | Flyable |
| N314BG | 44-73140 | 'Petie 2nd' | P-51D-25NA | | Based UK | Flyable |
| G-BTCD | 44-73149 | | P-51D-25NA | Mark Hanna | Duxford England | Flyable |
| N51MR | 44-73163 | | P-51D-25NA | Randall Kempf | WA/CO | Restore |
| N3751D | 44-73206 | 'Hurry Home Honey' | P-51D-25NA | Charles Osborn | Sellersburg IN | Flyable |
| CF-IKE | 44-73210 | 'Miracle Maker' | P-51D-25NA | Ike Enns | Tulsa OK | Flyable |
| N6328T | 44-73254 | 'Buster' | P-51D-25NA | Don Weber | Baton Rouge LA | Restore |
| N5428V | 44-73264 | 'Gunfighter' | P-51D-25NA | CAF | Omaha NE | Flyable |
| N/A | 44-73279 | | P-51D-25NA | Bob Baker | OK | Restore |
| N119H | 44-73275 | 'Never Miss' | P-51D-25NA | James Elkings | Salem OR | Flyable |
| N151SQ | 44-73282 | | P-51D-25NA | Square One Aviation | Chino CA | Restore |
| N951M | 44-73287 | 'Worry Bird' | P-51D-25NA | Michael George | Springfield IL | Flyable |
| N151MD | 44-73323 | | P-51D-25NA | Marvin Crouch | Encino CA | Restore |
| G-SIRR | 44-73339/44-74008 | | P-51D-25NA | David Gilmour | UK | Flyable |
| N33FF | 44-73350 | 'Archie' | P-51D-25NA | Lee Maples | Vichy MO | Flyable |
| ZK-PLI | 44-73420 | 'Miss Torque' | P-51D-25NA | Tim Wallis | New Zealand | Flyable |
| N51KD | 44-73436 | 'American Beauty' | P-51D-25NA | Brian Reynold | Olympia WA | Flyable |

| Civil Reg. | Military serial | Name | P-51 type | Owner/operator | Current base | Status |
|---|---|---|---|---|---|---|
| N2051D | 44-73454 | 'This Is It' | P-51D-25NA | Richard Bjelland | Stockton CA | Flyable |
| N4151D | 44-73458 | 'TF-660' | P-51D-25NA | William Hane | Mesa AZ | Flyable |
| N351D | 44-73463 | 'Oklahoma Miss' | P-51D-25NA | Bob Baker | Alva OK | Flyable |
| N6526D | 44-73415 | 'VooDoo' | P-51D-25NA mod | Bob Button | Dixon Ca | Flyable |
| N5483V | 44-73518 | 'Precious Metal' | P-51D-25NA mod | Don Whittington | Fort Lauderdale FL | Flyable |
| N151TP | 44-73543 | 'Sweetie Face' | P-51D-25NA | Tom Patten | Nashville TN | Flyable |
| N5478V | 44-73574 | | P-51D-25NA | Richard Ransopher | Kernersville NC | Restore |
| N2151D | 44-73656/ 44-12473 | 'Moonbeam McSwine' | P-51D-25NA | Vlado Lenoch | La Grange IL | Flyable |
| N35FF | 44-73693/ 44-13253 | 'Risky Business' | P-51D-25NA | Bill Rheinschild | Van Nuys CA | Flyable |
| N6168C | 44-73704 | 'FF-704 ' | P-51D-25NA | Lewis Shaw | Breckenridge TX | Flyable |
| N51BS | 44-73822 | 'Lil' Margaret' | P-51D-25NA | Butch Schroeder | Danville IL | Flyable |
| N10601 | 44-73843 | 'Old Red Nose' | P-51D-25NA | CAF | Midland TX | Flyable |
| N7TF | 44-73856 | 'Susie' | P-51D-25NA | Tom Friedkin | Chino CA | Flyable |
| N7098V | 44-73871 | 'Stephanie' | P-51D-25NA | Mustang Air Inc. | UK | Flyable |
| N167F | 44-73877 | 'Old Crow' | P-51D-25NA | Anders Saether | Oslo Norway | Flyable |
| N151DP | 44-73973/ 44-10755 | 'Cottonmouth' | P-51D-25NA | David Price | Santa Monica CA | Flyable |
| N51TH | 44-73990 | 'Alabama Hammer Jammer' | P-51D-25NA | Tom Henley | Emelle AL | Flyable |
| N51KB | 44-74009 | 'Kat Bird' | P-51D-25NA | Bill McGrath | | Flyable |
| N6519D | 44-74012 | | P-51D-25NA | James Smith | Kalispell MT | Flyable |
| N51U | 44-74204 | | P-51D-25NA | K.Shell | | Restore |
| N5466V | 44-74230 | | P-51D-30NA | Jack Rousch | MI | Restore |
| N151KM | 44-74311 | 'RCAF 577' | P-51D-30NA | Ken McBride | Hollister CA | Flyable |
| N64824 | 44-74389/ A68-175 | 'Speedball Alice' | P-51D-30NA | Art Vance | Sonoma CA | Flyable |
| N351MX | 44-74391 | | P-51D-30NA | Chris Woods | AZ | Restore |
| N151RJ | 44-74404 | 'Dazzling Donna' | P-51D-30NA | Bob Odegard | Kindred ND | Flyable |
| N51RT | 44-74409 | 'Donald' | P-51D-30NA | Robert Tullius | Sebring FL | Flyable |
| N6327T | 44-74417 | 'Donna-Mite' | P-51D-30NA | Richard James | Fennimore WI | Flyable |
| N64CL | 44-74423/ 44-10216 | 'Miss Van Nuys' | P-51D-30NA | Clay Lacy | Van Nuys CA | Flyable |
| N11T | 44-74425 | 'Damn Yankee' | P-51D-30NA | Tom van de Meullen | Lelystad Holland | Flyable |
| F-AZSB | 44-74427 | 'Nooky Booky IV' | P-51D-30NA | Baudet ·JCB Aviation | Nimes France | Flyable |
| N4132A | 44-74445 | 'Sugar Booger' | P-51D-30NA | Bill Hubbs | Pecos TX | Flyable |
| N1451D | 44-74446 | | P-51D-30NA | Nathan Davis | Indiana | Flyable |
| N74190 | 44-74452 | | P-51D-30NA | Millennium Classics | New York NY | Restore |
| N251HR | 44-74453/ 44-13903 | 'Glamorous Gal' | P-51D-30NA | Howard Ross | Wukegan IL | Flyable |
| N351DM | 44-74458' | Sizzlin' Liz' | P-51D-30NA | David Marco | Ft Lauderdale FL | Flyable |
| N10607 | 44-74466 | 'Barbara Jean' | P-51D-30NA | Harry Barr | Lincoln NE | Flyable |
| N1251D | 44-74469 | | P-51D-30NA | Classic American Aircraft | Chino CA | Flyable |
| N6341T | 44-74474 | 'Old Crow' | P-51D-30NA | Jack Rousch | Livonia MI | Flyable |
| N51GP | 44-74483 | | P-51D-30NA | George Perez | Sonoma CA | Flyable |
| N72FT | 44-74494 | 'Iron Ass' | P-51D-30NA | Hugh Bikle | Hollister CA | Flyable |
| N6320T | 44-74497 | 'Quicksilver' | P-51D-30NA | Bob Jepson | Kissimmee FL | Restore |
| N351DT | 44-74502 | 'Kentucky Babe' | P-51D-30 TF conv | Dick Thurman | | Flyable |

| Civil Reg. | Military serial | Name | P-51 type | Owner/operator | Current base | Status |
|---|---|---|---|---|---|---|
| F-AZJJ | 44-74506 | | P-51D-30NA | Rene Bouverat | France | Flyable |
| N151HR | 44-74524 | 'Dakota Kid' | P-51D-30NA | Henry Reichert | ND | Flyable |
| N991R | 44-74536 | 'Miss America' | P-51D-30NA | Brent Hisey | Bethany OK | Flyable |
| N51JT | 44-74582 | 'Crusader' | P-51D-30NA | Joe Thibodeau | Denver CO | Flyable |
| N3580 | 44-74602 | | P-51D-30NA | Jack Hovey | Ione CA | Flyable |
| N51RH | 44-74739 | 'Ole' Yeller' | P-51D-30NA | John Bagley | Rexburg ID | Flyable |
| N251KW | 44-74813 | 'Cripes A'Mighty' | P-51D-30NA | Ken Wagnon | Danville IL | Restore |
| ZK-TAF | 44-74829 | 'Rudolph' | P-51D-30NA | Graeme Bethell | Auckland NZ | Flyable |
| N8677E | 44-74865 | 'My Sweet Mary Lou' | P-51D-30NA | Gene Mallette | Blackfoot ID | Flyable |
| N6306T | 44-74878 | | P-51D-30NA | Tom Wood | Indianapolis IN | Flyable |
| N151BP | 44-74908 | | P-51D-30NA | Robert Pond | Palm Springs CA | Flyable |
| N6395 | 44-74923 | | P-51D-30NA | | Lelystad Holland | Restore |
| N51DK | 44-74962 | | P-51D-30NA | Fort Wayne Air Service | | Restore |
| N651JM | 44-74976 | 'Obsession' | P-51D-30NA | Jefferey Michael | Salisbury NC | Flyable |
| N5448V | 44-74977 | | P-51D-30NA | Christopher Gruys | Sante Fe NM | Flyable |
| N541OV | 44-74996 | 'Dago Red' | P-51D-30NA | Terry Bland | Mojave CA | Flyable |
| N3451D | 44-75007 | 'Paull' | P51D-30NA | Paul Poberezny | Oshkosh WI | Flyable |
| N51TC | 44-75009 | 'Rosalie' | P-51D-30NA | Ted Contri | Carson City NV | Flyable |
| N96JM | 44-75024 | | P-51D-30NA | War Eagles Museum/J Macquire | Santa Teresa NM | Restore |
| N2869D | 44-84390 | 'Section Eight' | P-51D-25NT | Doug Driscoll | American Falls ID | Flyable |
| N55JL | 44-84615 | 'Cloud Dancer' | P-51D-25NT | Jimmy Leeward | Ocala FL | Flyable |
| N51TF | 44-84658 | 'The Friendly Ghost' | P-51D-25NT | John Macquire | Santa Teresa NM | Flyable |
| N851D | 44-84745 | 'Crazy Horse' | P-51D-25NT | Stallion 51 | Kissimmee FL | Flyable |
| N251BP | 44-84753 | 'The Vorpel Sword' | P-51D-25NA | Bernie Jackson | Minden NV | Flyable |
| N850AH | 44-84850 | 'Su Su' | P-51D-25NT | Anderson Aviation | St Augustine FL | Flyable |
| N327DB | 44-84860 | 'Lady Jo' | P-51D-25NT | Daryl Bond | Chino CA | Flyable |
| N4223A | 44-84864 | | P-51D-25NT | Mike Coutches | Hayward CA | Flyable |
| N51YZ | 44-84900 | 'NACA 127' | P-51D-25NT NACA mod. | Bill Allmon | Las Vegas NV | Flyable |
| N201F | 44-84933 | | P-51D-25NT | John Mark | Oshkosh WI | Flyable |
| N210D | 44-84952 | | P-51D-25NT | Charles Monthon | Wilmington DE | Flyable |
| N7715C | 44-84961/ 44-73053 | 'Wee Willy II' | P-51D-25NT | Steve Hinton | Chino CA | Flyable |
| N51WT | 45-11391 | 'Nervous Energy V' | P-51D-30NT | Wally Sanders | Manassas Apt VA | Flyable |
| N51UR | 45-11471 | 'Diamondback' | P-51D-30NT | Bob Jepson | Kissimmee FL | Flyable |
| N921 | 45-11507 | 'Cripes A'Mighty 3rd' | P-51D-30NT | Kermit Weeks | Polk City FL | Flyable |
| G-MSTG | 45-11518 | 'Janie' | P-51D-30NT | M Hammond | UK | Flyable |
| N151AF | 45-11525 | 'Val Halla' | P-51D-30NT | Bill Anders | Eastsound WA | Flyable |
| VH-FST | 45-11526 | 'The Flying Undertaker' | P-51D-30NT | Rob Poynton | Australia | Flyable |
| N151W | 45-11540 | 'Excalibur' | P-51D-30NT | Jim Reed | Chesterton IN | Flyable |
| N51VF | 45-11553/ 45-11571 | 'Shangri-La' | P-51D-30NT | Mustang Air Inc. | New York NY | Flyable |
| N451DK | 45-11558 | | P-51D-30NT | DK Warbirds | Las Vegas NV | Flyable |
| N51MX | 45-11559 | 'Mad Max' | P-51D-30NT | Max Chapman | Kissimmee FL | Flyable |
| N5441V | 45-11582 | 'Spam Cam' | P-51D-30NT | Ed Maloney | Chino CA | Flyable |
| N151X | 45-11628 | 'Ho Hun' | P-51D-30NT | William Hane | Mesa AZ | Flyable |
| N151MW | 5-11633 | 'Lady Alice' | P-51D-30NT | Bob Jepson | Kissimmee FL | Flyable |
| N11636 | 45-11636 | 'Stang Evil' | P-51D-30NT | Michael Bertz | Broomfield CO | Flyable |
| N/A | 43-? | | P-51A | Gerry Beck | ND | Restore |
| N4451C | N/K | | P-51D | Ken McBride | San Martin CA | Restore |

# Appendix 4
# Mustang Models

Fortunately for modellers of all scales, the NAA P-51 Mustang is well covered. The first models of this classic came into existence in the mid 1940s for the purposes of aircraft recognition. When the production of aircraft kits began in the late 1950s, the Mustang was one of the earliest releases. Since then models have ranged in scale from the tiny 1:144 specimens to the mighty 1:24 offering from Airfix. Between these two points there is a plethora of kits, most being in the the dominant scales of 1:72 and 1:48. For the modeller determined to make his aircraft individual, there are many third-party add-ons that cover both detailing parts and decals.

| Manufacturer | Code | Scale | Model | Remarks |
|---|---|---|---|---|
| Academy | AC2132 | 1:72 | P-51D Mustang | USAAF |
| Accurate Miniatures | ACM3402 | 1:48 | P-51A Mustang | 311thFG |
| | ACM3418 | 1:48 | P-51B Mustang | G4-B |
| | ACM3419 | 1:48 | P-51C Mustang | 530thFS/311thFG |
| ARII | AR331 | 1:48 | P-51D Mustang | USAAF |
| Airfix | AX02083 | 1:72 | P-51B Mustang | 354thFS/355thFG |
| | AX02098 | 1:72 | P-51D/K Mustang | 249Sqdn/Swed AF |
| | AX05104 | 1:48 | P-51D Mustang | RAF/RNZAF/Swed AF |
| | AX14001 | 1:24 | P-51D Mustang | USAAF/RCAF |
| Classic Airframe | CF426 | 1:48 | P-51H Mustang | USAF |
| Condor | C7216 | 1:72 | A-36A Apache | 27thFBG 86thFBG |
| | CN7215 | 1:72 | P-51 Mustang IA | RAF |
| Doyusha | DOY1830 | 1:32 | P-51D Mustang | Old Crow |
| Hasegawa | HA00186 | 1:72 | P-51D Mustang | Blue Nose |
| | HA09377 | 1:48 | P-51D Mustang | resin parts |
| | HA00279 | 1:48 | P-51B Mustang | G4-N 'Geronimo' |
| | HA08115 | 1:32 | P-51D Mustang | 'Glamorous Glen' |
| | HA09362 | 1:48 | P-51D Mustang | 12FBS/18FBG Korea |
| | HAAP011 | 1:72 | P-51B Mustang | VF-T,B7-E,QP-M |
| | HAJT030 | 1:48 | P-51D Mustang | USAAF |
| | HASS15 | 1:72 | P-51D Mustang | USAAF |
| | HAST005 | 1:32 | P-51D Mustang | USAAF |
| | HA09411 | 1:48 | P-51D Mustang | 'Man O War' |
| | HA09393 | 1:48 | P-51D Mustang | 'American Beauty' |
| Hobbycraft | HC1321 | 1:72 | F-82 Twin Mustang | USAF |
| | HC1516 | 1:48 | P-51D Mustang | Shark Mouths |
| Historic Plastic Models | HIPM4805 | 1:48 | P/F-51H Mustang | USAF |
| High Planes | HPM7215 | 1:72 | P-51A Mustang | USAAF |
| | HPM7223 | 1:72 | P-51H Mustang | USAAF |
| | HPM7229 | 1:72 | Mustang X | Merlin prototype |
| | HPMR7201 | 1:72 | RB-51 Mustang | 'Red Baron' |
| | HPMR7203 | 1:72 | P-51 Mustang | 'Precious Metal' |
| | HPMR7204 | 1:72 | Learstang | 'Vendetta' Mustang |
| | HPMR7207 | 1:72 | Griffon Mustang | World Jet |
| High Planes | HPMR721 | 1:72 | P-51D Mustang Racer | 'Roto Fini' |
| High Planes | PMR7216 | 1:72 | A-36A Mustang | NX4E Race no 15 |
| | HPMR4801 | 1:48 | Griffon Mustang | World Jet |
| | HPM7223 | 1:72 | P-51H Mustang | USAAF |
| ICM | ICM48121 | 1:48 | P-51C Mustang | USAAF |
| | ICM48122 | 1:48 | P-51B Mustang | USAAF |
| | ICM48123 | 1:48 | Mustang Mk III | RAF |
| | ICM48151 | 1:48 | P-51D-5 Mustang | USAAF |
| | ICM48152 | 1:48 | Mustang Mk IV | RAF |
| | ICM48153 | 1:48 | P-51D-15 Mustang | USAAF |
| Italieri | IT0090 | 1:72 | P-51 Mustang I | Razorback |
| | IT0086 | 1:72 | P-51D Mustang | 12thFBS,65Sqdn, RNZAF |
| Monogram | MG0067 | 1:32 | P-51D Mustang | Phantom |
| Model News Company | MNC72005 | 1:72 | Mustang P-51H | USAF/ANG |
| Minicraft | MC14417 | 1:144 | P-51D Mustang | USAAF |
| Modelcraft | MCT48020 | 1:48 | F-82B Twin Mustang | 'Betty Jo' |
| MPM | MPM72085 | 1:72 | P-51A Mustang | photo recon |
| Revell | RV4167 | 1:72 | P-51B Mustang III | RAF |
| | RV4182 | 1:72 | P-51B Mustang | USAAF |
| | RV4133 | 1:72 | P-51B Mustang III | RAF |
| | RV4137 | 1:72 | P-51B Mustang | USAAF |
| | RV477351 | 1:32 | P-51B Mustang | USAAF |
| Seminar | SMA0132 | 1:32 | RB-51 Mustang Racer | 'Red Baron' |
| | SMA1572 | 1:72 | P-51D Mustang | USAAF |
| Tamiya | TA60749 | 1:72 | P-51D Mustang | 'Petie 2nd' |
| | TA60754 | 1:72 | F-51D Mustang | 18th FBG Korean War |
| | TA61040 | 1:48 | P-51D Mustang | 8th Air Force |
| | TA61042 | 1:48 | P-51B Mustang | USAAF |
| | TA61044 | 1:48 | P-51D Mustang | 18th FBG Korean War |
| | TA61047 | 1:48 | RAF Mustang III | Malcolm hood |
| Testors | TES590 | 1:48 | P-51D Mustang | USAAF |

# Appendix 5
# Mustang Books

As befits such a famous and significant aircraft it is no surprise that the Mustang and the people concerned with it have been covered well in the field of aviation literature. Numerous fighter aces of World War Two wrote memoirs, while their careers and aircraft have been written about and depicted exhaustively in monographs and histories. Mustang units, especially those in the 8th Air Force, have had histories written, while numerous technical studies concentrating on the design and development of the P-51 have appeared. Below is listed a broad selection for those who would like to know more about the classic American fighter of World War Two.

## P-51 Mustang Aces

To Fly and Fight: Memoirs of a Triple Ace   Col. C. E. 'Bud' Anderson and Joseph P. Hamelin   Pacifica Press; ISBN: 0935553347

Mustang Ace: Memoirs of a P-51 Fighter Pilot   Robert J. Goebel   Pacifica Press; ISBN: 0935553037

George Preddy, Top Mustang Ace   Joe Noah, Samuel L. Sox Jr   Preddy Memorial Foundation; ISBN: 0966904214

Mustang Aces of the 9th, 15th Air Forces & RAF   Mark Styling, Jerry Scutts   Motorbooks International; ISBN: 1855325837

Mustang Aces of the Eighth Air Force   Jerry Scutts   Osprey Pub Co; ISBN: 1855324474

Herky!: The Memoirs of a Checkertail Ace   Herschel H. Green   Schiffer Publishing, Ltd.; ISBN: 0764300733

## P-51 Mustangs In Service

Checkertails: The 325th Fighter Group in WWII   Ernest R. McDowell   Squadron/Signal Publications; ISBN: 0897473167

Mustangs & Unicorns: A History of the 359th FG   Jack H. Smith   Pictorial Histories Publishing Co; ISBN: 1575100290

Angels, Bulldogs & Dragons: the 355th Fighter Group   Bill Marshall   Champlin Fighter Museum Press; ISBN: 0912173025

F-51 Mustang Units Over Korea   Warren Thompson   Osprey Pub Co; ISBN: 1855329174

Air Force Colors Volume 3: Pacific/Home Front   Dana Bell   Squadron/Signal Publications; ISBN: 0897473760

Mustangs Over Korea: The F-51 Mustang at War 1950-1953   David R. McLaren   Schiffer Publishing, Ltd.; ISBN: 0764307215

## P-51 Mustang History

P-51 Mustang: A Photo Chronicle   Larry Davis   Schiffer Publishing, Ltd.; ISBN: 0887404111

P-51 Mustang Warbird History   Robert F. Dorr; ISBN: 076030002X

Mustang Designer: Edgar Schmued and the P-51   Ray Wagner   Smithsonian Institution Press; ISBN: 1560989947

P-51 Mustang   Gardner N. Hatch and Frank H. Winter   Turner Publishing Co; ISBN: 1563110806

NAA P-51 Mustang: Production Line to Frontline   Michael O'Leary   Osprey Pub Co; ISBN: 1855327031

P-51 Mustang The Operational Record   Robert Jackson   Smithsonian Institution Press; ISBN: 1560982535

P-51 Mustang Survivors/Restoration   Motorbooks Intl (Short Disc); ISBN: 1870601467

P-51 Mustang Warbird Tech Series   Frederick A. Johnsen   Voyageur Press; ISBN: 093342468X

## P-51 Mustang in Pictures

P-51 Mustang Nose Art Gallery   John M. Campbell and Donna Campbell   Motorbooks International; ISBN: 0879387823

P-51 Mustang: from the RAF to the Mighty Eighth   Michael O'Leary   Osprey Pub Co; ISBN: 1855327147

## P-51 Mustang Air Racing

Wet Wings and Droptanks   Birch Matthews   Schiffer Publishing, Ltd.; ISBN: 0887405304

Mustang The Racing Thoroughbred   Dustin W. Carter and Birch J. Matthews   Schiffer Publishing, Ltd.; ISBN: 0887403913

Speedsters: Today's Air Racers in Action   Phillip Handleman   Motorbooks International; ISBN: 0760303746

Reno Air Racing   Michael O'Leary   Motorbooks International; ISBN: 0760300844

And of course www.mustangsmustangs.com for all the latest Mustang news.

# Index

Page numbers in *italics* refer to illustrations

aerodynamic refinement 69, 72
Allison V-1710 engine 6–7, 8, 11, 77
Anderson, Captain Clarence Emil 'Bud' 42, 44
Arasmith, Lieutenant Lester 49–50
Australian Air Force, Royal 28, 68

Balfour, Paul 9, 10, 37
Beeson, Major Duane W 'Bee' 41–42
Blakeslee, Lieutenant-Colonel Donald 56–57, 58
bomber escort 21–22, 54, 55–56
bombing, daylight 53–54, 55
Boxer, USS 22, 24
Breese, Vance 8–9, 37
British trials and modifications 10–11, 14

Canadian Air Force, Royal 28, 29
canopy, tear-drop 17, 17
Cavalier Aircraft Corporation 20, 25–26, 25, 84, 85
    Turbo Mustang III 84–85
Chilton, R C 'Bob' 10, 37–38, 82
China-Burma-India Theatre of Operations 47, 49
Chinese Nationalist Air Force 32–33, 32

D-Day invasion operations 58–60
Drew, Lieutenant Urban L 41, 60

Far East service 62–63
French air force (*Armee de l'Air*) 28, 30
fuel tanks, external 21, 23, 57–58
fuselage 69, 72

Gentile, Captain Don 'Gentle' 38, 39, 40
Green, Lieutenant George 40–41, 43

Haitian Air Corps 36, 68
Harker, Ron 14
Hills, Pilot Officer Hollis H 38
Howard, Lieutenant-Colonel James H 48

Israeli air force 33–34, 66, 67, 68
Italian air force 28, 30

jet fighters 60, 62, 64

Kindelberger, James H 'Dutch' 5, 12, 15, 37
Korea 22, 24–25, 63–64, 66, 84
Korea, Republic of, Air Force 32–33, 32

Latin-American service 34–36, 34, 35, 36 see also Haitian Air Corps
Lend-Lease 12
Lockheed P-38 Lightning 54–55, 57
Lockheed YAH-56A Cheyenne 25–26, 84

McKennon, Major Pierce 'Mac' 40–41, 43
Mediterranean action 60–62
Meyer, General John C 42, 46, 48
Moore, Major Robert W 49

Netherlands East Indies air force 31–32
New Zealand Air Force, Royal 28, 29, 71
North American Aviation Inc. 5
    A-36A Apache 11, 12, 38, 60–61, 72
    F-6 Mustang 13, 20, 60
    F-6D 30
    F-51 Mustang 22, 23, 24–26, 25, 29
    F-51D 32, 33, 78, 84, 85
    F-51H 24, 75
    F-82 Twin Mustang 62, 63, 84
    F-82E 80, 83
    F-82F 68
    Mustang Mk I 10–12, 10, 18, 26, 27, 38, 62–63, 72
    Mustang Mk IA 12, 62–63, 70, 72
    Mustang Mk III 26, 27, 63, 70, 73
    Mustang Mk IV/IVA 26, 27, 78
    Mustang X 14
    NA-73X (P-51 prototype) 6–10, 6, 7, 8, 69
    P-51 Mustang (early-build) 13
    P-51A 47, 56, 70, 73
    P-51B 23, 32, 39, 59, 65, 70
    P-51C 19, 23
    P-51D 17, 17, 57, 58, 67, 68, 71, 73, 74, 76
        15th Fighter Group (FG) 61
        361st FG 59, 76
        364th FG 66
        Air National Guard 64
        warbirds 41, 42, 43, 50, 51, 52
    P-51D-10-NA 71
    P-51D-20-NA 50, 51, 71, 78
    P-51D-25-NA 78
    P-51D-30NT 51
    P-51H 20, 63, 77, 77
    P-51K 17, 71, 76
    P-51L/M 77
    P-82 Twin Mustang 20, 83, 84
    P-82B 79, 82–83
    P-82C/D 78, 82
    P-82F 81, 83
    P-82G 83–84
    RB-51 'Red Baron' 52

RF-51 Mustang 25
TF-51 Mustang 78, 84
XP-51: 9, 12
XP-51B 15, 16
XP-51F 17, 76
XP-51J 17, 20, 77
XP-82 Twin Mustang 20, 81–82
XP-87: 15

Operations *Bout One* and *Dallas* 22, 24
Operation *Neptune* 58–60
overseas production 28, 81

Pacific service 22, 49
Packard-built Merlin engine 15–17, 57–58, 73 see also Rolls-Royce engines
Philippine Air Force 33, 33
Piper PA-48 Enforcer 20, 85–86, 86
post-war service 22, 25–26 see also Korea
Preddy, Major George 46, 48
production plants 16

radiator layout 7, 37, 72
reconnaissance 26, 60, 62 see also North American F-6 and RF-51 Mustangs
Republic P-47 Thunderbolt 54, 56, 57
Rolls-Royce engines 5, 14–15, 57 see also Packard-built Merlin engine
Royal Air Force requirements 5–6
Royal Air Force service 10, 12, 14, 18, 26, 27, 28, 56, 70, 78

South African Air Force 28, 29, 63–64, 66
Swedish Air Force, Royal (*Flygvapnet*) 31, 31, 74
Swiss air force 31

tactical missions 56–57
trials airframes 80–81

US Army Air Force 12, 21–22
    4th Fighter Group (FG) 39, 40–42, 67
    8th Air Force 21, 53, 56, 58
    9th Air Force 56, 58–59
    332nd FG 'Tuskegee Airmen' 45, 61
    352nd FG 48, 71
    357th FG 23, 42, 44, 50
    361st FG 41, 59, 76
    530th FBS 49–50

warbirds 50, 52, 68
wing, 'laminar flow' 6, 37, 69

Yeager, General Charles 'Chuck' 44, 46, 46, 60